WHAT IS JOURNALISM FOR?

"A blend of expert knowledge and astute analysis on this pressing topic. If you care about democracy, you'll want to read it."
Margaret Sullivan, Columbia University Graduate School of Journalism

"An excellent book: a must-read for anyone who cares about or is interested in journalism."
Steven Barnett, University of Westminster

"A veritable feast of Jon Allsop! This great book serves up delicious insights about the nature of journalism and its future."
Joel Simon, Craig Newmark Graduate School of Journalism at CUNY

"Jon Allsop acknowledges journalism's flaws yet defends its necessity. Through vivid examples from Myanmar, the US and the UK, he illustrates how journalism's commitment to seeking and sharing truth is more vital than ever – especially amid democratic erosion and technological disruption."
Sheila S. Coronel, Columbia University Graduate School of Journalism

"A powerful call to action for journalists and citizens alike to defend democratic values and protect the vital role of journalism in shaping a just and informed society."
Laurent Richard, investigative reporter and founder of Forbidden Stories

The status quo is broken. The world is grappling with a web of challenges that could threaten our very existence. If we believe in a better world, now is the time to question the purpose behind our actions and those taken in our name.

Enter the What Is It For? series – a bold exploration of the core elements shaping our world, from religion and free speech to animal rights and the war. This series cuts through the noise to reveal the true impact of these topics, what they really do and why they matter.

Ditching the usual heated debates and polarizations, this series offers fresh, forward-thinking insights. Leading experts present groundbreaking ideas and point to ways forward for real change, urging us to envision a brighter future.

Each book dives into the history and function of its subject, uncovering its role in society and, crucially, how it can be better.

Series editor: George Miller

Visit **bristoluniversitypress.co.uk/what-is-it-for** to find out more about the series.

Available now

WHAT ARE ANIMAL RIGHTS FOR?
Steve Cooke

WHAT IS COUNTERTERRORISM FOR?
Leonie Jackson

WHAT IS CYBERSECURITY FOR?
Tim Stevens

WHAT IS HISTORY FOR?
Robert Gildea

WHAT IS JOURNALISM FOR?
Jon Allsop

WHAT IS THE MONARCHY FOR?
Laura Clancy

WHAT ARE MUSEUMS FOR?
Jon Sleigh

WHAT ARE THE OLYMPICS FOR?
Jules Boykoff

WHAT IS PHILANTHROPY FOR?
Rhodri Davies

WHAT ARE PRISONS FOR?
Hindpal Singh Bhui

WHAT IS VEGANISM FOR?
Catherine Oliver

WHAT IS WAR FOR?
Jack McDonald

WHAT ARE ZOOS FOR?
Heather Browning and Walter Veit

Forthcoming

WHAT IS ANTHROPOLOGY FOR?
Kriti Kapila

WHAT ARE CONSPIRACY THEORIES FOR?
James Fitzgerald

WHAT IS DRUG POLICY FOR?
Julia Buxton

WHAT IS FREE SPEECH FOR?
Gavan Titley

WHAT IS HUMANISM FOR?
Richard Norman

WHAT IS IMMIGRATION POLICY FOR?
Madeleine Sumption

WHAT ARE MARKETS FOR?
Phillip Roscoe

WHAT IS MUSIC FOR?
Fleur Brouwer

WHAT ARE NUCLEAR WEAPONS FOR?
Patricia Shamai

WHAT IS RELIGION FOR?
Malise Ruthven

WHAT IS RESILIENCE FOR?
Hamideh Mahdiani

WHAT IS SPACE EXPLORATION FOR?
Tony Milligan and Koji Tachibana

WHAT ARE STATUES FOR?
Milly Williamson

JON ALLSOP is a journalist who lives in London. Since 2017, he has written about the media for the *Columbia Journalism Review*, a New York-based magazine; during the same period, he has also covered British, French and international politics for publications including *The New York Review of Books*, *The New Yorker*, *The Atlantic*, *Vanity Fair* and *The Guardian*. From 2017 to 2020, he contributed to Gaming the Lottery, a transnational investigative project focused on the global lottery industry, from both the US and South Africa. He is a three-time finalist in the Mirror Awards for US media reporting and has served as a juror for the Pulitzer Prizes.

WHAT IS JOURNALISM FOR?

JON ALLSOP

First published in Great Britain in 2025 by

Bristol University Press
University of Bristol
1–9 Old Park Hill
Bristol
BS2 8BB
UK
t: +44 (0)117 374 6645
e: bup-info@bristol.ac.uk

Details of international sales and distribution partners are available at
bristoluniversitypress.co.uk

© Jon Allsop 2025

British Library Cataloguing in Publication Data
A catalogue record for this book is available from the British Library

ISBN 978-1-5292-3855-6 paperback
ISBN 978-1-5292-3856-3 ePub
ISBN 978-1-5292-3857-0 ePdf

The right of Jon Allsop to be identified as author of this work has been asserted by him in accordance with the Copyright, Designs and Patents Act 1988.

All rights reserved: no part of this publication may be reproduced, stored in a retrieval system, or transmitted in any form or by any means, electronic, mechanical, photocopying, recording, or otherwise without the prior permission of Bristol University Press.

Every reasonable effort has been made to obtain permission to reproduce copyrighted material. If, however, anyone knows of an oversight, please contact the publisher.

The statements and opinions contained within this publication are solely those of the author and not of the University of Bristol or Bristol University Press. The University of Bristol and Bristol University Press disclaim responsibility for any injury to persons or property resulting from any material published in this publication.

Bristol University Press works to counter discrimination on grounds of gender, race, disability, age and sexuality.

Cover design: Tom Appshaw

For Dad, Maddy and Sarah – and for Mum, who won't get to read this book, but whose footprints walk through it.

CONTENTS

List of Figures		xii
Acknowledgements		xiv
1	**Introduction**	1
2	**Democracy**	21
3	**Judgement**	43
4	**Criticism**	69
5	**Community**	92
6	**Beyond**	118
Notes		143
Further Reading		157
Index		161

LIST OF FIGURES

1.1	Map of modern-day Myanmar (iStock.com/PeterHermesFurian)	3
1.2	Taylor Swift on the set of *Good Morning America* for the launch of her album *Red*, 22 October 2012. Photograph by Paolo Villanueva (paolopv.com)	9
2.1	A seventeenth-century London coffeehouse (public domain)	22
2.2	Then-US president Barack Obama meets Myanmar's pro-democracy leader Aung San Suu Kyi in Yangon, 14 November 2014. State Department photograph by William Ng (public domain)	34
2.3	An anti-abolition mob attacks the warehouse that housed Elijah Lovejoy's printing press in Alton, Illinois, 7 November 1837. Lithograph (frontispiece) from John F. Trow's *Alton Trails* (New York, 1838), Library of Congress Prints and Photographs Division, Washington, DC (public domain)	38
3.1	Walter Lippmann at his desk, Los Angeles, 1936, originally published in the *Los Angeles Times*. UCLA Library Special Collections.	47

LIST OF FIGURES

     Copyright the Regents of the University of
     California. Reproduced under CC BY 4.0 licence
3.2 Ida B. Wells. Albumen silver print by Sallie E.   57
     Garrity. National Portrait Gallery, Smithsonian
     Institution. Reproduced under CC0 licence
4.1 Martin J. Dooley (right) by E.W. Kemble, from   70
     Mr Dooley's Philosophy by Finley Peter Dunne
     (William Heinemann, 1900) (public domain)
4.2 'The Plumb-pudding in danger'. Etching by   87
     James Gillray published by H. Humphrey, 1805
     (public domain)
5.1 A British newsstand, August 2024. Photograph   98
     by George Miller. Reproduced under CC
     BY 2.0 licence
5.2 Wa Lone (left) and Kyaw Soe Oo onstage at   114
     the Committee to Protect Journalists' annual
     International Press Freedom Awards on
     21 November 2019 in New York City.
     Photograph by Dia Dipasupil/Getty Images.
     Reproduced under CC BY 2.0 licence
6.1 The author on the final day of his internship   119
     at *BuzzFeed News* in New York City in 2017.
     Photograph by Megan Paolone (reproduced
     by permission)

ACKNOWLEDGEMENTS

Thanks go, first and foremost, to all those who gave up their time to share their thoughts with me for this book – particularly to my interviewees from Myanmar, for whom talking openly about the value of independent journalism is not without risk. Ali Fowle was of tremendous help in sharing her experiences in Myanmar and connecting me to others willing to do likewise. Thanks also go to George Miller, who trusted me to write my first book and edited it meticulously, as well as the rest of the team at Bristol University Press. Makana Eyre and Rebecca Schuetz took the time to read drafts and offer generous feedback, as did Michael Allsop, Maddy Allsop and Sarah Staples. Kyle Pope, my former boss at the *Columbia Journalism Review*, saw enough in me to set me on my current path writing about the media; without him, and other cherished colleagues past and present, this book would never have happened. Finally, thanks to Sarah Staples, for keeping me sane, and to Plymouth Argyle Football Club, for taking my mind off the book every so often (if definitely *not* keeping me sane).

1
INTRODUCTION

Around 3 a.m. on 1 February 2021, a friend phoned Kira Naing, a journalist in Myanmar, to tell her there had been a military coup. The country – which is also known as Burma, and which stretches from its border with China in the north to the Andaman Sea in the south – had been under military rule for most of its history after declaring independence from British colonizers in the 1940s, but for a decade or so, it had been in the throes of a promising, if fragile, transition towards democracy. Suddenly, in the early morning hours, it looked as if that might be coming to an end.

Kira Naing got to work. She woke her editors, then called a spokesperson for the National League for Democracy, a civilian party co-founded by the internationally renowned democracy campaigner Aung San Suu Kyi, that had effectively shared power with the military since winning elections in 2015. The spokesperson confirmed that a coup was taking place and that Aung San Suu Kyi had been arrested, then put the phone down as a car pulled up outside his house.

Around 6 a.m., Kira Naing's internet went down. She walked around her neighbourhood in Yangon, Myanmar's largest city. She visited a tea shop, a traditional venue for sharing information, opinions and gossip, and found locals talking in hushed tones, discussing withdrawing their money from cash machines and stocking up on bags of rice. People 'went into survival mode', Kira Naing recalled. Eventually, she figured out that the internet was still working in luxury hotels. She decamped to one of those to get the story of the coup out to the world.

The coup didn't come entirely out of the blue – military leaders had recently dropped hints at a press conference in Naypyidaw, the capital – but it was nonetheless a shock, especially for many young people. Kira Naing had grown up under military rule; when she was a child, her family told her to keep her head down and would speak Aung San Suu Kyi's name only in whispers. But when she became a journalist in 2015, civil liberties, including freedom of the press, were arguably at a high-water mark.

That freedom was far from absolute. Kira Naing had been forced to leave Myanmar before, after officials targeted her employer with lawsuits; when the coup happened, she had an emergency bag ready to go. Still, she couldn't believe that something so drastic was taking place in the 21st century. Initially, she didn't process the gravity of the situation as she worked long days reporting on the coup and popular protests that

INTRODUCTION

Figure 1.1: Map of modern-day Myanmar

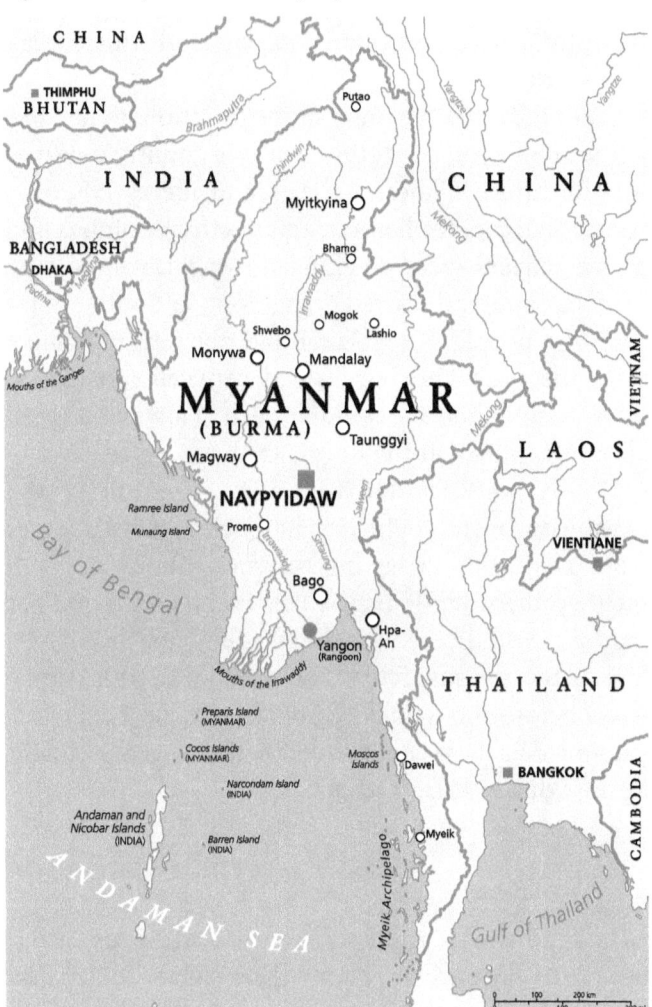

swelled against it. 'It was a very difficult situation as a victim of the coup, but it was a very exciting situation for journalists as well', she said. 'I was angry, I was frustrated, I was very sad, but I put all this energy into work.'

Eventually, the enormity of the situation hit her. She felt scared – for her future, for her country's future, for the future of her nephews and nieces. She was concerned, too, for her immediate safety. Soldiers and police officers were cracking down with increasing brutality and had started going door to door at night arresting people. Kira Naing had not returned home since the coup, moving instead between safehouses, but she still found she couldn't sleep. 'I always worried about the knock at the door', she said.

Finally, she decided to leave the country. She reasoned that she could keep in touch with her sources from afar, without having to worry about her own security and other logistics. Her friends reassured her that she would be back within a few months, maybe a year. But she suspected that it would be at least five years before she would be able to return. 'I was very pessimistic', she recalled. 'I knew that we cannot fight against this well-trained military.'

***

Kira Naing was right to worry – after an initial period of uncertainty about their rights, journalists quickly learned that the military junta intended to take a sledgehammer to Myanmar's independent press. Major news outlets had their licences to operate revoked. Dozens of media workers were imprisoned on spurious charges. (As of December 2023, only China, an authoritarian regime that does not tolerate critical media, was keeping more journalists behind bars than Myanmar.[1]) Some reporters said they were tortured in detention. One later alleged that soldiers told him to rape a woman in another cell, then raped him when he refused.[2]

Within a year, at least three reporters had died in incidents involving the military or in custody. Pu Tuidim had been covering clashes involving resistance fighters in a region bordering India and Bangladesh when soldiers abducted him along with several other civilians. The soldiers reportedly used the civilians as human shields against resistance fighters, then executed them. According to a representative of a resistance group, when Pu Tuidim's body was found, his limbs had been broken and his face mutilated.

Many journalists quit the profession. Hundreds of others fled into exile. Many went to Thailand; others scattered further afield. Some stayed in Myanmar, in borderlands controlled by armed rebel groups fighting the junta. Like Kira Naing, they continued to document what was happening inside their country. But finding and verifying facts at a distance was not easy. Just reaching people was hard due to widespread internet outages; when they could be contacted, even civilians and fighters opposed to the junta could be reluctant to talk, fearing detection or, in the latter case, loss of strategic advantage or reputational damage should abusive conduct of their own come to light. Journalists also struggled to balance their professional responsibility not to take sides with the fact that the junta had effectively waged war on them. Various journalists *did* openly take sides. Some outlets were accused of exaggerating the successes of the resistance, or of sensationalism.

At the same time, exiled journalists had to adapt to lives turned upside down: assimilating into new countries, with their different cultures, languages and prejudices; obtaining legal status (or facing the threat of deportation); finding healthcare; earning enough to survive. They reported struggling with exhaustion and survivors' guilt.[3] Cut off from many of their former revenue sources, the outlets that they worked for scrabbled to survive.

Still, through it all, independent journalism persisted. Exiled journalists found ways to push their work back inside Myanmar, where those hungry for news used technical tricks to circumvent ongoing curbs on the internet and social media. And some journalists remained inside junta-controlled areas while keeping a very low profile. Toe Zaw Latt, a senior journalist at the independent media company Mizzima, told me in 2024 that his outlet was operating a 'one foot in, one foot out' strategy: reporters inside Myanmar gathered facts, producers based in Thailand packaged them into stories, and those stories were then blasted back into Myanmar.

Toe Zaw Latt was also running a school for Myanmar-based journalists in a secret location in the jungle near the border between Myanmar and Thailand. 'There is a need to train especially a post-coup, new generation of journalists', he said. Demand was high. Some of those who attended the school had already worked as professional reporters. Others had served as citizen journalists, or 'CJs' – civilians who stepped up to find and share information as their professional counterparts went underground or fled. After the coup, they became 'one of the key players' in the media landscape, Toe Zaw Latt told me.

Many observers questioned whether these citizen journalists had the professional skills to gather information reliably and without showing bias; on the flip side, they were often paid poorly or not at all for their labour and in some cases reported mistreatment or exploitation by bosses.[4] But the desire of many citizens to help shape their country's future at a pivotal moment – by picking up pens, not guns – was unmistakable. As the prominent journalist Aye Chan Naing put it one year on from the coup, it was as if 'the whole country has become a journalist'.[5]

***

In September 2023, Gannett, the biggest chain of local newspapers in the US, posted an unusual job listing: for a reporter whose full-time role would be to cover the pop superstar Taylor Swift. (The company advertised for a full-time Beyoncé reporter, too.) At the time, Swift was ubiquitous: a music writer at *The Atlantic* described her as 'close to being the only monocultural phenomenon we have';[6] a journalist at *The Guardian* tried to avoid hearing about her for a month, and failed.[7] Gannett said it was looking for 'an energetic writer, photographer and social media pro who can quench an undeniable thirst' for 'content' about Swift. An executive at the company told a reporter that creating such roles is 'how we save local journalism'.[8]

The listing touched off a lively debate among American journalists. Some saw the Swift position as dumbing down and a sign of misplaced priorities; in recent years local newsrooms in the US have suffered dramatic cutbacks, including to their coverage of staples like city government and sport. In such a climate, how could spending money to cover a pop star be justified – let alone a means of *saving journalism*?

Other observers (myself included) were intrigued. Journalists have traditionally been called upon to scrutinize people in positions of power, and in recent years, Swift had become one of the most powerful people on earth, at least financially and culturally. When she encouraged her fans to register to vote, they (apparently) did so en masse; when her wildly popular 'Eras Tour' rolled into a city, it was typically credited with turbocharging the local economy. I and others feared, though, that whoever Gannett hired to cover her might not interrogate this power so much as churn out viral clickbait for Swift's hordes of online fans, while avoiding anything that might upset them.

Either way, applications flooded in, both from experienced journalists – including, Gannett said, a

INTRODUCTION

Figure 1.2: Taylor Swift

Taylor Swift on the set of the TV show *Good Morning America* for the launch of her album *Red*, 22 October 2012.

'very established' reporter covering the White House in Washington, DC – and Swift fans with blogs or active presences on social media. In the end, the job went to Bryan West, a self-professed 'Swiftie' who had worked for a local TV station in Phoenix, Arizona. The hire was controversial on several grounds. For starters, West is a man. Some online critics suggested Gannett should have hired a woman. Exploring girlhood and womanhood is central to Swift's music.

Others debated whether West was a big enough Swift fan for the job, or, conversely, might be too much of one to cover her without bias. In his application video, West included a photo of himself posing happily with Swift and pointed to the virality of one of his posts about her on social media. But he also insisted that he could report on her 'objectively'. (As proof, he listed three songs he hates: 'It's Nice to Have a Friend', 'Stay Stay Stay' and 'False God'.) 'I would say this position's no different than being a sports journalist who's a fan of the home team', West said after he was hired. He suggested that he intended to dig into the 'seriousness' of Swift's impact on 'society and business and music'.[9]

Several media critics made it clear that they intended to hold West to this promise. In November 2023 – on the day that the Earth's average recorded surface temperature exceeded 2 degrees Celsius above pre-industrial levels for the first time – Swift went ahead with a concert in Brazil in conditions of extreme heat. One of her fans passed out and later died of heat exhaustion. Questions were raised as to how Swift had handled it and whether enough water had been available. Swift has also been criticized for contributing to climate change by using private jets.

In the days afterwards, West published several stories about the incident, including an interview with an expert in crisis management. (Later, he also wrote about Swift's climate impact.) But his coverage mostly stuck to well-established facts about what had happened and Swift's official response. One writer suggested that fans of Swift had contributed better journalism in their social-media posts than West had via his established news organization.[10] Not that this was necessarily his fault. In an essay published on Substack the week after the concert, the journalists Frankie de la Cretaz and Nicole Froio blamed Gannett.

INTRODUCTION

West 'reportedly came into the job with two pages worth of story ideas that he wanted to explore', they wrote. 'So far, he's been used as nothing more than a glorified aggregator of social media posts.'[11]

* * *

A couple of weeks later, the American magazine *Time* named Swift its 2023 'person of the year'. Swift rarely gives interviews to journalists, instead communicating with her fans directly through social media channels and her music, while also cultivating a certain mystique. But she did speak to *Time* for a profile linked to the accolade. The author, Sam Lansky, emphasized her deftness at using traditional and new media to craft a public image, describing her as 'the master storyteller of the modern era'.[12] Lansky wrote that he had been tempted to challenge Swift on a part of her mythology that didn't appear to him to be true, but thought better of it. 'Who am I to challenge it, if that's how she felt?' he asked.

Some readers were quick to point out that challenging powerful people's feelings is precisely a journalist's job. But digging behind Swift's meticulous self-presentation is genuinely difficult. Nor is this problem limited to Swift: in the 21st century, journalists need their audiences to click on stories about celebrities more than celebrities need journalists to get those stories out to the world. Frequently, this distanced relationship has turned toxic, with celebrities, including Swift, lashing out – often fairly, often not – at media coverage they see as bigoted, cruel or voyeuristic. (In 2023, Swift's lawyers threatened action against a student who uses publicly available data to track celebrities' private flights on social media, accusing him of 'stalking and harassing behavior'.) Sometimes stars have worked their displeasure with media coverage into their art. The cover for Swift's tellingly titled 2017 album, *Reputation* – which was released following a spell of rocky headlines about her personal life – features an overlay of newspaper print that, on closer inspection, consists of her name repeated over and over.

As 2024 dawned, Swift was arguably the best-known person on the planet and at the same time fundamentally unknowable: an object; a canvas; the aggregate of a million distant impressions, including from members of the media. Right-wing commentators spread outlandish conspiracy theories about her politics, claiming that shadowy forces had roped her into a 'psyop' with the aim of throwing the 2024 US presidential election to the Democratic Party. Most of the commentary around her was less ridiculous – and less sinister – but amounted to little more than projection.

Writing about Swift's Eras Tour for *The New York Times Magazine*, the celebrated novelist and culture journalist Taffy Brodesser-Akner described 'the way this concert has consumed the world' as the 'living embodiment of one destabilizing question … How could I interpret Taylor Swift better than she does, better than her fans do online, every day, without my interference or input?'[13]

INTRODUCTION

* * *

In many ways, the experiences of journalists covering a brutal military junta and those covering the world's biggest pop star could not be more different. But they face some common challenges – including in the theoretically basic (yet actually very complicated) task of finding factual information and making it heard in an increasingly noisy world. Celebrity journalism is typically not an existential pursuit. But some reporters in the US *have* faced physical threats in recent years amid a broader uptick in attacks on the integrity of the press as a whole, not least from President Donald Trump and his indictments of so-called 'fake news'. (When Swift came out with a new album in 2024, the US magazine *Paste* left the author's name off a scathing review that it published, citing 'threats of violence from readers who disagreed' with its criticism of a prior release.[14])

Anti-media violence is a global story, from Slovakia to Gaza via Cameroon and Pakistan. Five years before Swift was named *Time*'s person of the year, that designation was shared by threatened journalists whom the magazine dubbed 'guardians' in a global 'war on truth'. Those honoured included the staff of *The Capital Gazette*, an American newspaper where five employees had recently been assassinated by a gunman who had previously sued the paper for defamation. Also included were Wa Lone and Kyaw Soe Oo, two reporters for the international news agency Reuters who were unjustly jailed in Myanmar.[15]

Journalists everywhere are also confronted by subtler questions as to what their work is *for*. Are they obliged to be unbiased in an age of strong opinions and high stakes, and if so, how? Whose voices should they represent, and whose stories should they tell? Who even gets to call themselves a journalist, and why? Classically, journalists have often seen themselves as trained professionals who go out into the world, gather facts about it without fear or favour, then write them down (or speak them aloud, or illustrate them) for a lay audience. But 'journalism' is a more capacious concept than that; its boundaries fuzzy, its purpose up for debate.

This has always been the case. During the English civil wars of the 1600s, early periodicals mixed military news with polemics, sensational stories and astrology; officials of the time expressed concern about the spread of 'false news'. But the question of journalism's purpose feels particularly acute now, at a moment when democracy is under threat across the globe, the spectre of disinformation – be it crude and manmade, or sophisticated and machine-produced, or some hybrid – feels ever-present and the business models that have traditionally supported for-profit news are collapsing. It is the question this book will take up.

In researching this book, I asked around two dozen journalists from Myanmar, the US and the UK what they think journalism is for. They offered a range of responses. Some said that journalism should speak truth to power – not only those in government but anyone who wields power over someone else. Others said that journalism must transmit information to the people as a basis for collective decision-making – but one said that, in an age of abundant information online, journalism is less about informing people than providing them with a 'common reference point'. I heard that journalism exists to give communities a voice and to fulfil the human need to tell stories, for the present and for posterity – and also that journalism should aim to materially improve people's lives. One respondent said that journalism can help those making it have fun and those consuming it kill time, much like playing a board game would. Others think (without necessarily endorsing the idea) that its purpose is to make money, either for its own survival or to confer riches, power and prestige on its owners.

All these responses are plausible, even when they seem contradictory. It is, indeed, impossible to reduce the question to a single easy answer. When I asked Jack Shafer, a veteran observer of the American media scene, what he thinks journalism is for, he suggested that I may as well have asked him 'Why is there physics?' The question, he said, 'is kind of an Everest of questions', its foundations 'buried in so much bedrock and magma' that it becomes 'a very heavy question to wrap your head around'.

Establishing what journalism is for first requires establishing what journalism *is*, itself no small feat. I favour a broad working definition: one that includes so-called 'straight' news but also opinion and analysis; that makes room for 'just the facts' newswire stories, florid magazine articles, everything in between and some things beyond. Journalism can excavate the past – as *The New York Times Magazine* did with its '1619 Project', a bold (and controversial) reframing of American history around slavery and its legacy – or take radically experimental forms, as the French TV channel TF1 did in 2022, when an interview with the singer Stromae about his mental health morphed into a concert that blurred the boundaries between journalism and performance art.

Sometimes, as the 20th-century US Supreme Court justice Potter Stewart once put it, you know journalism only when you see it. (Okay, Stewart was talking about pornography, but the same principle applies.) The word 'journalism' is itself often wielded as a statement of affirmation, conferring subjective approval or dismissal. Different observers might describe the same article as an exemplary piece of journalism, or not journalism at all.

This book is *my* answer to the question *What is journalism for?*, textured with the perspectives of my interviewees from Myanmar, the US and the UK. This is not an academic inquiry or survey; nor is it a practical textbook or ethics manual. It is, in its fashion, a work of journalism itself.

To the extent that I focus on three countries more than others, I've chosen them, respectively, for reasons of familiarity – I was born and live in the UK but studied journalism in the US and still write mostly for the American press – and a desire to step beyond my comfort zone. (I have written about Myanmar's media before, but do not consider myself an expert.)

INTRODUCTION

I certainly don't claim that these countries represent some scientific sample of journalism cultures. (Indeed, cross-country comparison is a limiting prism through which to view journalism, as we will see.) My perspective is defined by who I am (a straight white British man in his early thirties) and who I've chosen to speak with (and the barrier of language, especially in the case of Myanmar). This book is to some extent biased towards the Western-facing media debates that I have been steeped in for many years, even as it tries to situate those debates in a global context.

Even allowing generously for subjectivity, however, I still believe that the question of what journalism is for needs an answer, or *answers*, and that those cannot be so subjective as to lose all meaning. In searching for them, I've tried to tread a path between the realm of abstract ideas and the constraints of the real world. This book will recognize how plutocratic owners and the influence of money often corrupt journalism, without becoming a manifesto against the evils of the ownership class. It will raise the dangers of disinformation and the loss of trust in traditional news without claiming to solve either problem. And it will acknowledge how changes in technology – from the invention of the printing press to the rapid development of artificial intelligence (AI), currently the biggest perceived disruptor to the news business – have affected journalism, without becoming a book about the potential of the latest technological fad to turn journalism on its head. In part, that is because key questions, not least around the impact of AI, lack clear answers at time of writing. But it is also because the idea of journalism has, over hundreds of years, proven itself much bigger – and more resilient – than its often ephemeral mechanics of ownership, production and delivery.

In this book, I'll pursue the question of what journalism is for by examining what I see as its three main functions. Journalism must judge what is true (Chapter 3). It must engage in constant critical thought (Chapter 4). And it must do so about, and on behalf of, a given community – of geography, of identity, of interest, or all of the above – that is ultimately an inseparable part of a wider world (Chapter 5). These functions exist in a close, if in many ways nuanced, relationship with democracy, which is the focus of the next chapter. And they cannot exist at all without the support of other societal institutions, which are the focus of Chapter 6.

These principles, of course, are not exhaustive. But they do, as I see it, combine to form a spirit that is identifiably and distinctively journalistic. At their simplest, they boil down to the idea that journalism is one way, and perhaps the most important way, that a society talks to and examines itself.

* * *

This is a book of its time. I do not yet know whether Donald Trump won re-election to the White House in 2024 – at time of writing, a gunman had just tried to assassinate him and the Democrats had just switched out their candidate to face him, turning the race on its head – nor whether Myanmar's junta collapsed under growing pressure. Nor is my own relationship with journalism static: it has evolved from my early, very green days editing a student newspaper in London through journalism school in New York (where I dreamed of becoming a hacky political reporter) to an unusual transatlantic perch as a London-based freelance journalist writing mostly about the media for the *Columbia Journalism Review*, a New York-based magazine (for which, among other things, I often criticize hacky political reporting).

In my career to date, I've done investigative journalism – digging into the lottery industry in the US, and how some players have been able to win big prizes hundreds of times despite astronomical odds – and international reporting, spending a few months in South Africa in 2018; since then, I've written hundreds of pieces of analysis, commentary and magazine-style reportage. I am, hopefully, now old and experienced enough to have a nuanced view of journalism, but still young enough not to be totally disillusioned by it. In any case, this book is my answer to the question of what journalism is for, *now*.

One thing that never changes is the importance of the question itself. Whatever you think journalism is or is for, whether you agree with my answers or not, it remains a powerful social institution – not to mention a powerful business, with its own hierarchies, injustices and financial interests – that deserves to be scrutinized and held to account, just as journalists do to other powerful actors.

In my time reporting on the media industry, I've sometimes heard that journalists *aren't the story* or don't have very much power at all; at least, not compared to the *good old days* when they were society's informational gatekeepers. Introspection can be uncomfortable. And journalists do lack power in important respects, as I will argue. But journalism remains the lens through which many people come to know and understand the world around them, whether they recognize that fact or not. Despite – or, more likely, because of – the sharp contemporary challenges to its form and relevance, interrogating journalism's purpose is perhaps a more vital task than ever.

2
DEMOCRACY

Humans have always had a 'hunger for awareness', as the journalism scholar Mitchell Stephens put it in his excellent *History of News*.[1] In the Greek agora and Roman forum, news was exchanged orally; in ancient Rome, written news was also displayed in public places and distributed to different arms of the empire. Throughout history, leaders of tribal and predominantly oral societies have disseminated word of current events that are important – or merely entertaining or unusual – in creative ways. When divisions emerged among members of the Hopi, a Native American people, at the turn of the 20th century, liberal and conservative factions chose different 'criers' to spread the news by word of mouth.

Today, we understand 'journalism' as something more than the sharing of 'news'. (If I text a friend the football scores, I am not generally thought to be engaging in journalism.) Nonetheless, the distinction is not a neat one delineating from some clean cut-off point. Rather, the modern definition of journalism – at least in the West, and the English-speaking world in particular – developed bit by bit, and in tandem with various assumptions that have always been challenged.

In their book *The Elements of Journalism*, Bill Kovach and Tom Rosenstiel trace what we think of as 'modern journalism' to early newspapers that emerged from the coffeehouses of 17th-century England.[2] (See Figure 2.1.) Printed news proliferated earlier, after the German inventor Johannes Gutenberg revolutionized the printing process in Europe by facilitating the mass reproduction of typeset text. (And Chinese and Korean inventors advanced this technology even before Gutenberg.) But it wasn't until the 17th century that news began to appear in regular publications that

Figure 2.1: A seventeenth-century London coffeehouse

London coffeehouses such as this one were important sites for the exchange of news.

contained a multitude of different stories and had their own brand or identity. Over time, Stephens writes, the press, and newspapers in particular, 'began to be thought of as synonymous' with journalism.[3]

As journalism evolved in the 17th century, so did related concepts. Rulers increasingly found themselves conscious of public opinion, even if they did not care for it. Advocacy journalism – using journalistic tools to push a given argument or cause – grew more sophisticated, as did outright propagandizing. Around the time of the English civil wars, one opportunistic publisher, Marchamont Nedham, by turns ran pro-royalist and pro-republican mouthpieces depending on which way the wind was blowing (or, perhaps, the pay).[4] And the modern liberal conception of freedom of the press began to be articulated. John Milton, who later wrote the epic poem *Paradise Lost*, outlined an argument for the principle in his influential 1644 tract *Areopagitica*, which argued against the system whereby publications were required to obtain an official licence (though he would later complicate this legacy by working as a licensor on behalf of Oliver Cromwell's regime).

The exchange of scientific correspondence also accelerated in this period, and with it a culture of verification – a principle that would come to be closely associated with journalism (as would the argument that journalists should adopt a scientific-type method). In the 1660s, the Royal Society began meeting in London. It adopted the motto *Nullius in verba*: 'Take nobody's word for it' (foreshadowing, perhaps, the modern journalistic cliché that if your mother says she loves you, you should check).

In 1695, licensing restrictions on printing in England lapsed. Around the same time, the word 'journalist' started to gain currency in English, according to the *Oxford English Dictionary*, though its first recorded usage of 'journalism' (a loan of the French word *journalisme*) didn't come until the 1830s, when the word appeared in the *Westminster Review*. During the same decade, the US began to see the growth of journalism as a mass-market, general-interest product, one funded by advertising and sold cheaply enough that non-elite readers could afford to buy it, in a climate of expanding literacy.[5] Around the same time, the electrical telegraph was invented, which would revolutionize the ability to communicate information by removing the need to transport it manually, while accelerating the commodification of journalism as a product.[6]

To sell news to the widest possible spectrum of publications, incipient news agencies tried to keep partisan spin out of it, as well as avoiding locally or regionally specific language. These agencies, among others, engaged in the *reporting* of verifiable facts – part of an emerging 'journalistic method' that, as Stephens defines it, had three core components: *observing* events firsthand; *investigating* official accounts of them; and showing *enterprise* to seek out information about them before word of them arrived. In the 1820s, newspapers in New York sent boats into the harbour to source European news from arriving ships, first in collaboration with each other, then in competition. In 1835, the journalist and soon-to-be-novelist Charles Dickens raced by coach to deliver news from Devon to London ahead of a rival reporter.[7]

If English borrowed the word 'journalism' from French, the French language subsequently lifted the English meanings of the words 'reporter' and 'interviewer'; indeed, the communications scholar Jean K. Chalaby has argued that the norms of modern journalism – as a fact-oriented discipline, unadorned by commentary and literary flair – were a distinctively Anglo-American invention of the 19th century.[8] Over time, this type of journalism came increasingly to be seen as a vocation undertaken by dedicated, trained professionals. The mediums in which they worked expanded as communications technology continued to evolve, from print to radio, through the age of television and into the age of the internet, with its explosion of news sites, webshows, streaming services, podcasts and social media.

At time of writing, AI – which has developed to the point of being able to generate convincing prose, and even audiovisual media, from relatively unsophisticated human prompts – appears to be on the cusp of upending journalism again. Observers have debated whether this will be for better or worse. AI-powered tools have already started to help journalists simplify onerous tasks, like sifting through large datasets. But such tools threaten to replace at least some human journalists by working quicker without requiring a salary, and have the potential to crank out disinformation with even greater efficiency. Already, they have been accused of stealing and remixing journalists' work.

As I write this book – which blends fact, analysis and opinion, with (I hope) some nuance – it still isn't clear whether a machine might one day outperform my efforts. My best guess is that it will not because this type of writing is an essentially human task, one that requires feelings and critical faculties that a machine can't replicate. Future readers can ask their personalized AI servant what became of my career to find out if I was right.

***

If journalism has developed alongside changes in technology and news organizations' commercial and professional practices, it has also been seen as rising in tandem with modern democracy, and inseparable from it. Kovach and Rosenstiel spoke for many when they wrote that 'journalism has no claim on the public's attention other than in the name of democracy'.[9] Journalism, in this view, serves as a crucial tool in a people's ability to govern themselves, by ensuring the broad availability of the information needed for collective decision-making and by providing a way for people to hold their leaders to account. Democracy, for its part, guarantees the underlying conditions – speech rights, the rule of law – that enable journalists to do their jobs.

It is certainly true that journalism and democracy reinforce each other. But the relationship between them is not without nuance. In part, this is because the concept of democracy, like that of journalism, is a contested one with fuzzy boundaries. Definitions that focus above all on elections and the health of civic institutions – including a free press – can fail to take account of outcomes, such as the distribution of wealth and national cohesion, that bear on democratic success. Countries that are generally considered to be very established democracies often fall short on key indicators of democratic performance. No democracy on earth is anywhere close to perfect.

Perhaps the most useful way of thinking about democracy comes from the academic Laurence Whitehead, who argues that the concept must be 'floating but anchored', like a moored boat.[10] Reasonable observers can disagree substantially as to the meaning of the term, just as a moored boat can drift on the tide – but they may not untether the concept from certain immovable requirements, just as the moored boat cannot move out of range of its anchor. Russia, for example, has elections, but is not a true democracy given that it also imprisons, poisons and kills dissidents and muzzles independent media, including by jailing journalists on flimsy charges and branding reporters and their outlets as 'foreign agents', a stigmatizing label that also entails onerous paperwork. (Like their counterparts from Myanmar, many independent Russian outlets now operate from exile.)

The anchor analogy is also helpful when thinking about journalism:[11] reasonable observers can disagree as to the meaning of the term, but you cannot, for example, brazenly lie and still be a journalist. The analogy can also help us think about the relationship *between* journalism and democracy. If these two concepts are moored boats, then they are certainly in close proximity; they might even appear, from the surface, to be attached to the same anchor. But their anchors – the core spirit of each idea, in other words – aren't exactly the same.

Journalism can decline in democracies that otherwise appear healthy, as a result of a lack of commercial viability, for example. And it can survive in countries that few people would consider functional democracies. The authors of *Worlds of Journalism*, an ambitious 2019 survey of media workers in dozens of countries, argue that pinning the concept of journalism too tightly to that of democracy can reflect a 'Western bias'; not only has journalism 'always existed beyond democratic lands', they write, but it is still only consumed within democracies by a minority of the world's population.[12] The authors also point out that in parts of the Global South, journalism's *'raison d'être'* might not be democracy but economic development.[13]

Development and democracy, of course, are not mutually exclusive goals. And the same survey found that journalists around the world do 'broadly link the news media to the promotion of political self-governance by articulating support for such journalistic roles as being an informer, a watchdog, and a disseminator'.[14] If it might be overselling the relationship to conclude that journalism has 'no claim' on public attention if not in the name of democracy, the 'anchor' of the latter idea includes principles like self-determination and the diffusion of political power that are served well by journalism, and are likely, at least more so than any obvious alternative, to guarantee journalists' right to perform their core roles of truth-finding and critical thinking. Dictators prefer lapdogs to watchdogs.

This has certainly been the case in Myanmar – since the 2021 coup, and also at prior points in the country's recent history. Indeed, that history shines its own light on the complex, non-linear, but ultimately beneficial relationship between journalism and democracy, one that is distinctive, if not entirely separate from the ways in which that relationship developed in the West. It is a story of journalism finding a way forward even in painfully anti-democratic conditions. It is a story, too, of journalists engaging in a fight for more democracy, achieving it (at least for a while) and finding that its promise was not always fulfilled.

* * *

The first printing press in Myanmar was established by a US missionary. Its first newspaper was published by British officials, who colonized the country starting in the 1820s. And yet the story of Myanmar's media – and the idea of its freedom – is not merely one of Western importation. As British authorities came increasingly to censor the press, King Mindon, who ruled over a still-independent part of what is now Myanmar (which

Britain later annexed), enshrined press freedom in law, perhaps the first such statute in the wider region not to be imposed by outsiders. ('If I do wrong, write about me', Mindon declared.) The king later founded a newspaper that took aim at the pro-British bias of other papers.

In the early 20th century, newspapers in Myanmar often criticized British rule and advocated national independence, which was finally achieved in 1948. For a time after that, a diverse, often aggressive press built itself up, undergirded by a new constitution with liberal guarantees on free expression. But the space for that grew smaller, and in 1962, General Ne Win seized power in a coup. A brutal chill soon fell across the media environment. The new regime nationalized privately owned newspapers, then banned them. And it imposed strict pre-publication censorship.[15]

Military rule would last for decades. But the independent media landscape was not totally barren. Independent thinkers found subtle ways to slip their ideas past military censors; over time, more publications were authorized. In 1988, mass protests against the regime ushered in what one journalist later described as a 'brief, amazing period of press freedom'.[16] Employees of the state-controlled media, otherwise a source of propaganda, even evinced some degree of support for the protesters.[17] 'We publicly announced that we had left behind censorship and were now with the Burmese people', one editor recalled.[18]

Military rule was quickly restored, as was draconian censorship. But journalists would again cover important events despite official intimidation, including another significant wave of anti-regime protests in 2007, and a devastating cyclone the following year.[19] 'There were a lot of great local reporters doing a lot of important work', recalled Thin Lei Win, who covered the cyclone for Reuters while posing as a volunteer supporting the relief effort (and went on to found *Myanmar Now*, a news site offering in-depth coverage of the country). 'But they were also having to do it undercover or surreptitiously.'

Even when covering smaller everyday stories, journalists would probe the lines that the censors enforced. 'We pushed our boundaries', one of them, Nyein Nyein Naing, told me. 'We had to bargain with the censorship board very often, on a weekly basis.' On occasion, she and her colleagues would ignore its edicts and be hauled in for a dressing down.

While journalists like Nyein Nyein Naing tried, bit by bit, to create more space for independent media from inside Myanmar, others worked for exiled outlets that thrived in the years after the protests of 1988. Many of these outlets had ties to the pro-democracy movement and young activists who opted to leave the country after the protests were crushed.

Aye Chan Naing trained as a dentist but joined the movement and ended up in exile, from where he wrote a newsletter for a student-activist group documenting the regime's human rights violations. The self-styled democratic government-in-exile eventually selected him to help establish the Democratic Voice of Burma (DVB), a radio station based in Norway that broadcast into Myanmar from afar. The station relied on people discovering it through word of mouth. 'People tried to tune in because that was the only source for them to get independent news', Aye Chan Naing recalled; listeners would put up homemade antennae and move their radio sets around their homes for a better signal. Initially, DVB aired 'some propaganda' on behalf of the pro-democracy movement, Aye Chan Naing said, though over time it became more independent.

By the early 2010s, Myanmar's media sector was 'vibrant' if 'significantly restricted', as Lisa Brooten, Jane Madlyn McElhone and Gayathry Venkiteswaran put it in *Myanmar Media in Transition*, an indispensable book that they edited.[20] Around that time, the regime began to open up the country, and its media landscape along with it. Thein Sein, a former general who became president in 2011, started to speak about the press as the 'fourth estate', a term of Western origin commonly understood as an affirmation of the media's independence from government. Ye Htut, an official in the information ministry (who would become known as the 'Facebook minister' for his prolific posting on that platform), quipped that any journalists still wanting to be censored would have to go to neighbouring China.[21]

The persistence of threats to the press belied such rhetoric. But the regime did implement some concrete reforms. Officials unblocked websites including Reuters, the BBC and YouTube. Pre-publication censorship ended and private newspapers were permitted to publish on a daily schedule for the first time since the early years of Ne Win's rule. Outlets that had operated out of exile began to move home, despite some suspicions as to the regime's intentions. Aye Chan Naing met with the information ministry and 'could see how much they really wanted us to come back', he recalled. DVB did come back, but it maintained an operation in Thailand as a precaution. A few years later, it decided that it was safe to shut the Thai operation down.

Internet access, once sparse and heavily restricted, exploded, fuelled by a telecoms boom and the widespread adoption of smartphones. One result was the mass adoption of Facebook, which became a crucial platform for the delivery and consumption of news (so much so that it has been referred to as the 'digital tea shop'[22]). By the mid-2010s, the respected international watchdog Reporters Without Borders, which previously considered Myanmar one of the worst places on earth to be a journalist, had moved the country up more than 30 positions in its annual press-freedom rankings, above countries like Malaysia, Mexico and Turkey.[23] In 2016, Esther Htusan, a reporter from Myanmar who worked for the Associated Press news agency, won a Pulitzer Prize, the most prestigious award in American journalism, as part of a team that covered the abuse of slave labour, much of it from Myanmar, in the global seafood industry.

But these advances risked masking the challenges that persisted for Myanmar's media. Even at the high-water mark for press freedom, journalists were harassed, arrested and even, on occasion, killed. Following elections in 2015, the National League for Democracy

– spearheaded by Aung San Suu Kyi, a Nobel Peace Prize laureate and, to that point, darling of Western democrats – entered government. (See Figure 2.2.) This ought to have augured well for the consolidation of Myanmar's press-freedom gains. But it was ultimately a disappointment. Aung San Suu Kyi and some of her colleagues often treated journalists high-handedly or worse. The state continued to weaponize both old and new laws against the press, including through defamation and other provisions in a statute regulating online communications. And criticizing the military remained perilous.

Starting in 2017, Myanmar was the subject of international condemnation after Wa Lone and Kyaw

Figure 2.2: Barack Obama and Aung San Suu Kyi

Then-US president Barack Obama meets Myanmar's pro-democracy leader Aung San Suu Kyi in Yangon, 14 November 2014.

Soe Oo – the two reporters with Reuters, who were investigating atrocities against the minority Rohingya population in the state of Rakhine, which borders Bangladesh – were arrested after being entrapped into handling supposedly sensitive documents.[24] They were charged under the Official Secrets Act, a colonial-era law. While the pair had been reporting on the military and police, *The New York Times* later alleged that it was Aung San Suu Kyi – whose handling of the Rohingya crisis would cause her international reputation to fall off a cliff – that posed the biggest obstacle to their release.[25] (They were eventually freed as part of a broader amnesty of prisoners in 2019.) Htusan, meanwhile, fled Myanmar following a series of physical and online threats, including from a prominent supporter of Aung San Suu Kyi.[26]

And the widespread adoption of Facebook turned out to be a double-edged sword: it allowed people to exchange and consume news, but also violent vitriol. The Aung San Suu Kyi supporter threatened Htusan on his Facebook page, which at the time had some 300,000 followers. During the Rohingya crisis – which numerous international observers would characterize as a genocide – Facebook was widely accused of allowing itself to become a key vector of hate speech and incitement. (Globally, Facebook's algorithms have long been accused of rewarding inflammatory or otherwise emotive content to keep users hooked on the platform. At the time, Facebook took down various accounts connected to Myanmar's military and commissioned an independent review which found that it had not done enough to prevent the spread of hateful content, but also that it could not bring human rights to Myanmar by itself.[27])

Ahead of elections in 2020, Reporters Without Borders described press freedom as 'the big omission' of Myanmar's decade-long transition towards democracy.[28] In early 2021, the military ended that transition entirely. On the whole, the period was kinder on Myanmar's journalists than those that preceded and followed it. Too often, though, even those claiming the mantle of democracy during that time acted as if they did not see independent journalism as a core component of it.

* * *

If the relationship between journalism and democracy has not followed a straightforward trajectory in Myanmar, the same is true in the US, where it has fluctuated not just over time but across social divides and physical space as well. The First Amendment to the US Constitution – which was enacted in the years after the country's founding to guarantee the freedoms of expression, religion, assembly and the press, and which remains in force today – has helped shield the media from government interference. But in practice, threats to this freedom have recurred throughout US history, from the Sedition Act of 1798 – which criminalized 'false, scandalous and malicious writing' about the government (even if, in practice, this applied only to newspapers opposed to President

John Adams) – through to Donald Trump's crusade against 'fake news'.

And, if the US has historically been held up as an example of a strong democracy, it has not been a strong democracy for all its citizens. Until the Civil War of the 1860s, many Black Americans were enslaved; after that, they were denied basic economic and political rights and subjected to the persistent terror of racist violence, especially in the South. As Steven Levitsky and Daniel Ziblatt note in their book *How Democracies Die*, the norm of mutual partisan toleration that underpinned national-level US democracy for much of the 20th century rested on a terrible bargain: 'racial exclusion and the consolidation of single-party rule in the South'.[29] The scars of systemic racism, of course, remain visible today.

Journalists have been among the victims of these democratic disparities. In the 1830s, a mob murdered Elijah Lovejoy, a newspaper editor who advocated the abolition of slavery; papers associated with the two major political parties of the era suggested that he had brought his fate upon himself. (See Figure 2.3.) More than a hundred years later, reporters covering the surging civil rights movement in the South themselves faced shocking violence from racist mobs; one journalist, Paul Guihard of Agence France-Presse, was killed while reporting on a riot aimed at preventing the desegregation of the University of Mississippi. In 2020 – after a white police officer murdered George Floyd, a Black man in Minneapolis, sparking mass protests nationwide – police assaulted and arrested dozens of

Figure 2.3: Anti-abolition mob

An anti-abolition mob attacks the warehouse that housed Elijah Lovejoy's printing press in Alton, Illinois, 7 November 1837. Lovejoy was killed that night.

journalists who had turned out to cover the unrest. Omar Jimenez was arrested while reporting live on CNN. Linda Tirado, a photojournalist, was blinded in one eye by a police projectile. In 2024, it was reported that she was dying as a result of her injuries.

Over the years, many journalists have fought back against the failure to establish a thriving multiracial democracy in the US, be that by giving marginalized communities a voice in the press or by aggressively skewering the hypocrisy of politicians and the historically white-dominated mainstream media. During the Second World War, Black-owned newspapers led a 'double V' campaign to push for victory in the war but also true democracy and equality for Black Americans at home.[30] (Also during this period, Black newspapers were harassed by various branches of the US government, including the FBI.) After the war, various Black journalists became actively involved in the civil rights movement. In Alabama and Arkansas, for instance, newspaper editors ran their publications at the same time as leading local branches of the National Association for the Advancement of Colored People.[31]

In the present day, a debate is flaring among US media-watchers (myself included) as to whether the press as a whole should be more overtly pro-democracy in its coverage, a response to Trump's efforts to overturn his loss in the 2020 election – which resulted in his supporters staging a violent insurrection at the Capitol building in Washington – and to his profoundly anti-democratic rhetoric during his subsequent campaign to return to the presidency in 2024. At time of writing, the result of that election isn't known. The debate as to whether, and *how*, the media might better fight for democracy is sure to continue.

* * *

The relationship between journalism and democracy is a close one, with many intersections. But it is also messy and contingent. As we have seen, what we today consider to be journalism grew not as a flower out of the spreading soil of global democracy, but also in response to less romantic economic, technological, even psychological conditions. We certainly cannot say that the developed West has both democracy and journalism while the rest of the world has neither. As the *Worlds of Journalism* survey found, journalists in different places have different ways of conceiving of their work, its guiding professional ethics and its relationship to democracy.

The survey also found, of course, that journalists the world over broadly agree that the role of the news media is linked to 'the promotion of political self-governance'. When I asked Thin Lei Win, the journalist who covered the 2008 cyclone in Myanmar, whether journalism is seen there as having different values to elsewhere, she replied that in her view (and with some nuances), what it means to be a good journalist is universal, not a 'Western construct'. Dictatorial authorities trying to condition journalists to be obedient partners in their rule has had the opposite effect in Myanmar, she said, creating a class of 'seriously good muckraking journalists' who 'really want to find out what is behind policies and decisions'.

In a globalized world, boundaries between different journalistic cultures are porous. One country or bloc can influence journalism elsewhere – by exporting a state-funded broadcaster overseas, for example, or by paying out of their aid budgets to provide trainings and other support for journalists. (Both these trends have been visible in Myanmar, where many people who distrust state propaganda have turned over the years to broadcasters funded by, if editorially independent of, the governments of the US and the UK.[32]) Some big multinational corporations own news companies not only in different countries, but on different continents, allowing these subsidiaries greater or lesser measures of editorial independence.

If different people see journalism and its relationship to democracy differently, the variation is better understood not as being between countries, or blocs, but between countries *and* within them. Different newsrooms in a single country may have greatly diverging journalistic philosophies. Of course, these same divisions can play out within newsrooms as well. Indeed, an individual journalist may have very different views of their craft at different points of their career, as they change and the world around them changes, too.

Journalism can serve as a bulwark for democracy where it exists, and push to create, or reinstate, it where it does not, standing for the proposition that people should have a say both in who rules them and what information they get to consume about those rulers. A newspaper journalist in the UK (who wished to remain anonymous), told me that as he sees it, 'Journalism *is* democracy to a large extent' – if by democracy we mean not only the outcome of elections, but the deeper 'freedom to influence public debates and have views and express yourself'.

As I've argued here, I don't see journalism and democracy as conceptually interchangeable. But the distinctive spirit of journalism – to find and share the truth, and to criticize society in all its facets, on behalf of different types of community – is at least in some sense *democratic*, whether or not it's exercised explicitly in the name of democracy. This is particularly true of the first part of this equation, the notion of finding and sharing the truth, which is not typically handed down on stone tablets or in government press releases. Finding it is, often, a collective endeavour. And, like the broader relationship between journalism and democracy, it can be very messy indeed.

3
JUDGEMENT

In January 2017, the day after Donald Trump was sworn in as US president, Sean Spicer, his press secretary, told journalists a series of false claims about the size of the crowd at the inauguration. The following day, Chuck Todd, then the host of the venerable political show *Meet the Press*, asked Kellyanne Conway, another Trump spokesperson, why Trump had sent Spicer out to utter a 'provable falsehood'. Conway said that Spicer had merely offered 'alternative facts'. '*Alternative facts?*' Todd scoffed, incredulously. 'Four of the five *facts* he uttered were just not true. Look, alternative facts are not facts. They're falsehoods.'

Spicer's and Conway's remarks set the tone for the Trump administration's approach to the news media: one of unprecedented, often contemptuous dishonesty, not only around big scandals (which politicians of all stripes have always lied about), but everyday vanities and absurdities that were easily disprovable, or should have been. (At one point, reporters spent days trying to establish whether a dog Trump had honoured for its role in a raid targeting a terrorist leader in Syria was male or female.) 'Alternative facts' quickly became shorthand for fears that the US – and perhaps the entire world – had entered a post-truth age, in which the truth no longer mattered as much as what people wanted to believe.

The instinct of many journalists was to fight this drift. For their employers, this also proved an enticing commercial strategy, as Trump's victory fuelled an uptick in news consumption among at least part of the public (a trend known as 'the Trump bump'). CNN ran an advert promising 'facts first' and showing a picture of an apple. 'This is an apple', the voiceover intoned, even if 'some people might try to tell you that it's a banana'.

The invocation of 'alternative facts' offended the most basic idea that journalists have of their job. The *Worlds of Journalism* survey found that journalists everywhere see a duty to 'report things as they are' as one 'canonical' aspect of their work.[1] In their *Elements of Journalism*, Kovach and Rosenstiel describe journalism as 'a discipline of verification' whose 'first obligation is to the truth'.[2]

Some truths – the difference between an apple and a banana; the size of a crowd – are easy to establish and report. (Relatively speaking, anyway: while Spicer's claims about Trump's inauguration were wildly false, counting the precise number of people in a crowd can be complicated, especially if the crowd is big and people are slipping in and out of it.)

Many truths, though, are harder to pin down. Conway's invocation of 'alternative facts' may have shocked many American journalists, but something like the idea has echoed throughout history, and not just in the mouths of political hacks. Nearly a hundred years earlier, Ivy Lee, considered a founder of the modern field of public relations, said that stating an 'absolute fact' is 'humanly impossible': 'All I can do', he wrote, 'is to give you <u>my interpretation of the facts</u>'.[3] He wasn't necessarily being devious. If Kovach and Rosenstiel claim that the 'first obligation' of journalism is to the truth – and that there is 'absolute unanimity' as to this point – they also acknowledge that it inspires 'utter confusion'.

Kovach and Rosenstiel argue that journalists must deal in the 'practical or functional form of truth' by which society operates on a day-to-day basis, rather than any 'absolute or philosophical' standard – a journalist's truth, they note, is not that of a chemical equation.[4] This argument is itself a practical truth: journalists must try their best to make sense of the world around them, knowing that this is not an exact science. Their work otherwise risks dissolving into a soup of irresolution.

Yet even this more modest aim is fraught. It involves daily recalibration, negotiation and debate within journalists' societies, their places of work, even their own minds. In addition to what constitutes the truth, journalists must constantly think about where and how to find it, which truths we prioritize (in a world too full of facts for journalists to find them all), who gets to engage in such work and on what terms.

The debate around these questions is perennial, though it seems to cycle back with particular relevance at moments of elevated societal tension or change. It's unsurprising, then, that the debate has grown louder of late in many parts of the world, including both the US and Myanmar. The language of the debate differs from place to place and from person to person. Some strive for 'objectivity' or to avoid 'bias'. Others seek 'fairness' or 'balance'.

These terms are certainly not interchangeable, even if journalists can be prone to use them imprecisely. But they all orbit perhaps the most fundamental puzzle confronting any journalist: how they are supposed to engage with the truth and manage its elusiveness, amid their own – unavoidably human – convictions, doubts and anxieties.

* * *

The version of this debate that concerns 'objectivity' – the idea, broadly speaking, that a definite truth exists independently of people's subjective viewpoints, and that journalists should try their best to find it – is universally relevant here, even if many of its particulars are distinctively American. Perhaps the canonical text on objectivity was written in 1922 by Walter Lippmann, a famed US newspaper columnist and public intellectual. (See Figure 3.1.) Much of this book, *Public Opinion*, reads today as outdated and elitist. It argues, essentially, that a specialized class of technocratic insiders should be empowered

Figure 3.1: Walter Lippmann

Walter Lippmann in Los Angeles, 1936, originally published in the *Los Angeles Times*.

to propose policy based on data and expertise, given that the average citizen in a democracy has a warped understanding of the world around them.

But much of the book's diagnosis of this warped understanding reflects timeless concerns about truth and how we perceive it. For Lippmann, humans live in the real world but can't possibly see it in all its complexity, and so also construct a 'pseudo-environment' of mental images, symbols and stereotypes (a word, incidentally, that Lippmann coined in its modern usage). These are deeply flawed and yet shape our perception; this perception in turn affects how we act, which, of course, has consequences in the real world.[5] And so on.

Those in positions of power can shape this 'pseudo-environment' in our heads by controlling the flow of information, as can the news media, which Lippmann describes as our 'chief means of contact' with the world beyond our direct experience. Journalists choose what stories to cover in the first place; what is *news* and what isn't. When they go to the scene of an event that they (or their boss) have chosen to cover, they produce a story that is inevitably coloured by their preconceptions and impaired by their blind spots. Any individual story can be told countless ways. And when these individual stories are packaged together, the result is 'a whole series of selections as to what items shall be printed, in what position they shall be printed, how much space each shall occupy, what emphasis each shall have', as Lippmann writes. 'There are no objective standards here.'[6]

Lippmann was talking specifically about the newspaper. Today, we have more means at our disposal to see the world beyond our line of sight, including high-quality photography, TV footage and social media. But images, too, can deceive; sometimes, they are outright fakes. Even when they aren't, we can only see what the camera shows us. Whatever the medium, journalism – as the reporter Wesley Lowery argued in an influential op-ed published in 2020, nearly a hundred years after Lippmann – still sits 'atop a pyramid of subjective decision-making: which stories to cover, how intensely to cover those stories, which sources to seek out and include, which pieces of information are highlighted and which are downplayed'. He added, 'No journalistic process is objective. And no individual journalist is objective, because no human being is.'[7]

Not that Lippmann would subscribe to all of this – indeed, he advocated objectivity as a process, or the idea that humans, *because* they can't themselves be objective, must follow methodical steps to find the best available version of the truth. Lippmann was writing in an age of journalistic doubt and scepticism, driven, among other things, by the proliferation of propaganda during the First World War and the rise of the PR industry. (*All I can do is to give you my interpretation of the facts.*) If the idea of objectivity was popular in this period, it was not, as the journalism scholar Michael Schudson has put it, as 'the final expression of a belief in facts but the assertion of a method designed for a world in which even facts could not be trusted'.[8] A world, in other words, much like that of today, with its metastasizing war, propaganda and spin.

The debate around journalistic objectivity flared with particular insistence in the summer of 2020, following the police murder of George Floyd in Minneapolis. Critics, including Lowery, characterized the common journalistic understanding of objectivity as a racist product of years of white, often male dominance in newsrooms; in their view, it had become a code word for establishment beliefs and practices – including, but not limited to, taking statements from the police at face value, even when they were provable lies – that many industry leaders seemed to see as unquestionable standards of truth and neutrality. Defenders of objectivity countered that this argument missed the point – that objectivity is an *antidote* to the inevitability of subjectivity, one that is perhaps more necessary now than ever.

The battle lines thus drawn, the two sides in the debate frequently talked past each other. The critics – often (though by no means always) journalists of a younger generation – sometimes saw defenders of objectivity as fogies with a complacent attitude towards those in power, and as obstacles to diversity, representation and change in newsrooms. The defenders – often (though by no means always) journalists of an older generation – sometimes saw the critics as dangerous Jacobins bent on tearing down methodical, fact-driven journalism and replacing it with raw emotion and opinion. Along the way, the meaning of the term 'objectivity' got lost.

Each side often caricatured the other. Much of the time, they actually agreed that journalism should be rigorous, open-minded and transparent in its pursuit of facts, and that it should hold those in power vigorously to account. Prominent voices on both sides[9] claimed similar ideas for their cause, including Lippmann's.

There were some real theoretical disagreements, around, for example, whether it is realistic to expect people, who aren't objective, to design processes that are. ('While the scientific method may be designed to be impartial', my *Columbia Journalism Review* colleague Mathew Ingram wrote in 2020, 'it has also been used throughout history to justify some of the most horrific injustices'.[10]) The root of the debate, though, seemed to me to be more practical than conceptual, concerned less with objectivity as defined by Lippmann and others, and more with how it had come to be policed in many corners of the US media business.

* * *

In recent decades, major US news organizations, particularly print newspapers, have often positioned themselves as unbiased arbiters of the truth; as far back as 1896, the publisher of *The New York Times* famously promised to report the news 'impartially, without fear or favor, regardless of party, sect, or interests involved'. The paper still cites this as a core value today. But in the years after the US came into being, its press was often opinionated, and vituperatively so. One historian likened editors of the time to 'Vandals and Huns', slashing barbarically at each other in defence of their partisan interests.[11]

These days, as the historian Rick Perlstein told me in a 2020 interview, the ideology of the elite US media is more consensual; the journalists who ascend to the 'Empyrean heights' of the industry, Perlstein said, generally subscribe to the myth that 'Americans are united and fundamentally at peace with themselves'.[12] The evolution from Huns and Vandals to Empyrean heights didn't just result from the rise of objectivity as an abstract value in Lippmann's day, but from more concrete shifts in political culture and media economics. As newspapers became mass-market products funded by adverts aimed at broader swathes of society, they aimed to cultivate as wide an audience as possible. Publishing divisive political content was not considered the best way of selling the most things to the most people.

Wherever it came from, inoffensiveness crept into mainstream US journalism. (In the same breath as its 'without fear or favor' declaration in 1896, *The New York Times* promised 'language that is parliamentary in good society'.) In my work as a media critic, I've observed various manifestations of this in recent years. News organizations often balance the positions of rival political 'sides' in their coverage, treating them as equivalent even when the position of one has vastly more factual merit than the other. When covering Trump, journalists used euphemisms to describe his behaviour – labelling his racist statements as 'racially charged' and refusing to call his lies 'lies' – perhaps because they feared that plainer language would make it *sound like* they were taking a side.

At some point, the idea of objectivity also became a sort of shield for beliefs that inspire broad consensus among American elites; a coded means of taking subjective claims out of the realm of journalistic contestation. In the 1970s, the columnist Jack Newfield described these beliefs as including 'welfare capitalism, God, the West, Puritanism, the Law, family, property, the two-party system, and ... the notion that violence is only defensible when employed by the State'. Values change over time, of course. But at least some of these beliefs continue to inspire broad consensus in the highest echelons of the US news business today.

These shibboleths notwithstanding, US journalists have often been expected to adopt what the academic and media critic Jay Rosen has called the 'view from nowhere', or the idea, loosely speaking, that they must present the truth in ways that are perfectly impartial, stripped of any bias or preconceptions.[13] (Rosen borrowed the phrase from the philosopher Thomas Nagel.) In 2017, shortly after Kellyanne Conway sparred with Chuck Todd, Lewis Raven Wallace, a young transgender reporter at American Public Media, wrote a blog post in which he argued that objectivity was 'dead' and suggested that the best way for journalists to fight 'alternative facts' was by asserting strong values, including explicit opposition to racism, authoritarianism and transphobia.[14] Wallace was fired. He later wrote a book challenging the 'myth' of objectivity, titled, pointedly, *The View From Somewhere*.

Indeed, this mangled version of objectivity – a cocktail of journalistic rootlessness, inoffensiveness and adherence to elite norms – has often played out as a workplace dynamic within American journalism. In the 1930s, the Associated Press fired a reporter and union organizer, Morris Watson, citing dissatisfaction with his work. The Associated Press argued before the US Supreme Court that it had the right to decide which of its employees were too biased to work there. But the court ruled that Watson had been wrongfully fired for his labour advocacy.

More recently, journalists from oppressed backgrounds have reported bosses curbing their coverage of people with similar identities and life experiences on the grounds that it could be perceived as biased (even though being a white man is not seen as a disqualification from writing about other white men). Felicia Sonmez, a reporter at *The Washington Post* who has alleged that she was sexually assaulted in the past, was for a time banned from covering stories about sexual abuse. In 2020, in the hours after the basketball superstar Kobe Bryant died in a helicopter crash, Sonmez linked on social media to a news story about a historic rape claim against Bryant. The story was factual and she didn't add much commentary of her own, but the *Post*'s editor, Marty Baron, nonetheless accused her of hurting the paper's reputation and suspended her. (Of all the people American journalists are not supposed to offend, the recently deceased top the list.) She was reinstated after much of the newsroom protested. 'We have repeatedly seen colleagues – including members of management – share contentious opinions on social media platforms without sanction', the paper's union wrote. 'Here a valued colleague is being censured for making a statement of fact.'[15]

This incident exposed what I see as an irony in how many US newsrooms treat their employees in the 21st century. Often, bosses seem to encourage journalists to become recognizable public personalities with large followings on social media or regular spots as TV talking heads; walking adverts, in other words, for their employer's brand. And yet journalists, particularly those who aren't white men, have sometimes been censured for showing too much *personality*, in the individualistic sense of that term.

This is the context in which the debate over objectivity in US journalism must be understood. The term, as much as a philosophical abstraction about how journalists should seek the truth, is also about power: about who has it in society and in the newsroom, and who does not; about whose subjective speech is treated as normal journalism and whose is not; about the ends – selling news as a product, often – for the sake of which all this is enforced. Those who police the concept of objectivity do not hold the master key to understanding what journalism is for, any more than those who are policed are heretics.

Even if these power dynamics were stripped away, however, the task of finding the truth would remain one of perpetual, pointed contestation – and so questions that currently cannot be untangled from those of power *do* still matter in the abstract. If it's unavoidable that journalists will bring their subjective views and experiences to their work, is this an unfortunate inevitability to be mitigated? Or is it a source of richness to be embraced? Or can it be both? Can a journalist also be an activist, or vice versa? If so, when and for what? Can journalists approach their work through a moral prism? Should they?

At time of writing, the idea of approaching journalistic work with 'moral clarity' has become a particular point of controversy, especially in the US: what to some simply means telling the truth from a place of basic decency signifies to others a troubling, even arrogant, slide towards false certainty and unmitigated subjectivity. In their book, Kovach and

Rosenstiel describe moral clarity as 'a hallmark of extremism', and dangerous on such terms. 'If moral clarity is the goal, neo-Nazis would claim they have it', Kovach and Rosenstiel write. 'So would jihadists'.[16]

There are also signs that the grip of the consensual model of mainstream American journalism is starting to evolve into something more complicated. Nakedly partisan or ideological media – some of which is not very concerned with the truth at all – is surging, especially on the political right. US journalism is not yet back to the age of Vandals and Huns, but it seems to be getting closer. In 2023, Eric Levitz, then a writer at *New York Magazine*, suggested that if objective-style journalism is dying, it isn't at the hands of Jacobin journalists but because the advertising-supported business that long underpinned it – now dominated by big tech companies like Facebook and Google – is dying, too, and because too few people want to pay for it themselves.[17]

In 2021, Harry's, a company that sells razors, stopped advertising on a podcast produced by *The Daily Wire*, a hard-right media outlet, after a listener complained about its anti-LGBTQIA+ content. In response, the site created its own line of grooming products, dubbing them anti-'woke'. (In a video ad, its co-founder fired a flamethrower at a box marked 'Harry's'.) Executives claimed the line brought in nearly US$20 million in revenue in 2023. 'In order to win we have to rip the economy in two', the co-founder said.[18] Divisive political content had *become* a sales tool.

***

JUDGEMENT

There is a long tradition of activists – or, at least, people with a strong point of view – doing good journalism. Often, this point of view has provided an impetus, galvanizing a journalist to shine light on important facts that might otherwise have remained in shadow. As Wallace points out in *The View From Somewhere*, Ida B. Wells, a pioneering Black journalist, investigated the lynching of Black people in the US at the turn of the 20th century, campaigning to eliminate it while at the same time telling 'a factual story that was nowhere to be found in the pages of white papers'. (See Figure 3.2.) Decades later, crusading gay publications would lead the way in covering the AIDS crisis, at the same time as criticizing the denialist, homophobic

Figure 3.2: Ida B. Wells

coverage of the mainstream press.[19] Even defenders[20] of the more traditional understanding of journalistic objectivity acknowledge that 'advocacy journalism' can be worthwhile – they just don't want all journalism to look that way.

This is a fair concern. Yet even journalism that purports to be objective – or neutral, or unbiased, or straight down the middle – often makes an argument. The telling of a story in the first place implies that the author thinks the subject matter is true and important; the way a story is structured implicitly offers some interpretation of its content. 'The kind of work I do is inherently normative – *I think these things are wrong, and I'd like to do something about it*', the anonymous newspaper journalist in the UK told me. Even Baron, the former editor of *The Washington Post* and a stickler for objectivity, has argued that journalists are 'obliged to try to distinguish right from wrong' and that 'abuse of power is a clear and grievous wrong'.[21]

It is typically expected that even straight-news journalists will advocate for their own professional rights – freedom of the press from government interference, access to official information and so on – and, at least as it coincides with these rights, for the maintenance of democracy itself. Indeed, when democracy is under attack, journalism arguably becomes a form of activism. If one political 'side' is waging war on the truth, then telling it can be, or at least look like, a radical act.

This may make American journalists uncomfortable, but it does not appear to be an aberration globally speaking. The *Worlds of Journalism* survey found that respondents described their work in 'interventionist' ways – that is to say, in terms of advocacy for a mission or set of values – more strongly in societies that are experiencing upheaval.[22] At such moments, societies often grow polarized, and journalists are often expected to pick a side.

Unsurprisingly, this has been the case in Myanmar. Journalists there have testified over the years to pro-democracy politicians expecting loyalty from members of the press out of shared opposition to the military regime; journalists were expected to take sides, too, while covering state and communal violence against the Rohingya population in the 2010s.[23] Such demands have only grown since the 2021 coup. 'Being a journalist and being a media organization that reports independently on the situation in Myanmar does, in a way, make you part of a resistance to the coup', Thomas Kean, the former editor in chief of the independent news site *Frontier Myanmar*, told Voice of America in 2022. 'Your values and what you stand for are completely anathema to the regime.'[24]

Indeed, after the coup, many journalists from Myanmar seemed to view their role as being to hit back. 'I have dreamed before to be the fourth pillar. But now our aim is to fight the junta', the head of *Khit Thit*, a popular online outlet, said. 'This is to achieve press freedom again.'[25] One told the *Columbia Journalism Review* that journalists had become 'the mouthpiece of the resistance, and we are comfortable with that'.[26]

This is not how everyone sees their work, however. When I spoke to Thin Lei Win in 2023, she had just returned from visiting exiled journalists in Thailand. 'Independent media has done an amazing job under the most difficult of circumstances', she told me. Despite some biased journalism in favour of the resistance, many outlets have continued to scrutinize both the regime and the alternative government-in-exile, even though their conduct is 'absolutely not comparable', Thin Lei Win said. Many journalists, she added, are 'asking the difficult questions. They're holding power to account'.

The journalists from Myanmar with whom I spoke for this book (who do not, to be clear, constitute a representative sample of the country's media scene) generally seemed comfortable with the idea of advocating for democracy in an abstract sense. But they also clearly valued their independence from the groups fighting the junta, which have themselves often kept journalists at arm's length or deprived them of information.

In 2024, *Frontier Myanmar* reported on the 'vastly different media strategies' of different armed groups, noting that while some have stonewalled the press almost entirely, others have engaged more openly, including by allowing reporters from major Western outlets into their territory to chronicle the fight against the junta. Around the same time, however, even these authorities imposed new codes of conduct for journalists, banning them, in vague language, from undermining their governance and even suggesting that they might have to start wearing uniforms (though at time of writing, it isn't clear how strictly any of this has been enforced).

Officials from one group suggested that the codes were to ensure journalists' own safety, while a leader of another insisted that it wasn't trying to curtail reporting. 'The media, frankly, has helped the revolution a lot', the official said. 'And we understand that trying to control freedom of expression is not compatible with the democratic country we long for.' Still, various journalists expressed concerns that their freedom might be under threat, at a moment when various resistance groups were gaining in power and engaging in behaviour – including, in some places, alleged human rights abuses – that itself demanded journalistic scrutiny. 'All the armed forces want the media to promote them, to make propaganda for them', one journalist told *Frontier Myanmar*. 'If we don't do that, they don't like us.'[27]

* * *

Journalists sometimes guard the gates of their industry. They are typically advised to steer clear of joining political parties and protest movements, and even of posting their opinions on social media. (Some journalists don't even vote.) If such demands aim in part to preserve journalists' independence of thought, they also aim to preserve the societal *impression* that journalists are, as a group, trustworthy, neutral arbiters of the news.

Guarding the gates in the other direction, David Simon, a former newspaper reporter who went on to write *The Wire* and other hit TV shows, told a Congressional hearing in 2009 that 'citizen journalism' is an insult to the status of journalism as a specialized profession. 'A neighbor who is a good listener and cares about people is a good neighbor. He is not in any sense a citizen social worker', Simon said. 'A neighbor with a garden hose and good intentions is not a citizen firefighter.'[28]

At the time, a certain conception of the 'citizen journalist' – the notion that anyone could shine a light on the truth, armed with only a smartphone and an internet connection – was a romantic one. Since then, it has arguably lost its lustre across much of the West as the techno-optimism of the 2000s and early 2010s has faded. And yet, as we saw in the Introduction, citizen journalists have taken on a crucial, if by no means unquestioned, role in Myanmar in recent years, stepping up to help document the abuses of the regime as professional journalists have been relentlessly targeted. Citizen journalists have been targeted too, and in some cases have lost their lives.

This is not to say that citizen journalists should be a substitute for professionals or that the targeting of either is acceptable. Nor is it to say that cash-strapped news organizations should expect citizen journalists to work for meagre wages (as I was told has often been the case in Myanmar). But citizen journalists still have an important role to play, at least in some parts of the world – and everywhere, the boundary between 'citizens' and 'journalists' is hazy and porous. Professional journalists are citizens themselves. They have a stake in the society they live in just like everyone else. They have biases, identities, opinions and interests outside of work, because all humans do.

Non-professionals can produce journalism so long as they do so in accordance with its spirit. 'There is not a priestly class of people called "journalists" who are able to produce Certified Real Journalism, which exists on a higher plane from the tawdry musings of the rabble', the US commentator Hamilton Nolan wrote in 2019. 'If you find out true things and write them, congratulations: you're a journalist, at least for the length of that story. Journalism is an open door.'[29]

At the same time, a society having people who *do* pursue journalism as their full-time job – without exercising any sort of conceptual monopoly over the field – is essential. And it is probably for the best if these people avoid clear conflicts of interest that could undermine their ability to follow facts in a spirit of intellectual independence. A partisan operative is more than capable of doing a piece of journalism on the terms laid out by Nolan. But if journalism exists, in part, to hold partisan operatives to account, then relying on them to produce it is self-evidently flawed. Could a journalist theoretically run for political office and cover their own campaign in a spirit of honesty? Yes. Would it be reasonable to trust them to do so? Of course not.

If the lines here seem murky, it's because they are – they, too, are the product of daily negotiation that depends on all sorts of specific factors. A journalist who writes opinion columns can more justifiably rally behind a political candidate than one whose job is to hold that candidate to account (even if, in my view, the best opinion journalism is itself produced from a position of greater intellectual independence than partisan endorsements tend to allow). The reporter whose job is to hold a political candidate to account can more easily join a local theatre troupe than the local drama critic – though even this isn't to say that the latter couldn't join the troupe under any circumstances.

What is needed is for this daily negotiation to take place in good faith – and, ideally, transparently – between journalists and bosses who respect them as people, rather than seeing them as detached observers with no right to thoughts or feelings. Above all, deciding where the lines should lie requires sound judgement.

* * *

Journalism – rooted in an uncertain world; executed by often wonderful, always flawed human beings – must find avenues towards the truth, rather than giving up and saying it's too difficult, too fraught, too elusive. The process of getting there will never be perfect; indeed, the best journalism acknowledges its own shortcomings front and centre. But journalists have to try.

In doing so, certain principles, some of which we have encountered already, are useful. Open-mindedness. Humility. Rigour. Intellectual honesty. Independence, not from society or oneself, both of which are impossible, but as a form of self-awareness – the ability to stand back and identify trains of thought that block a mind from seeing the world as it is.

For me, all these ideas (and myriad others) come under the banner of *judgement*. In some ways, this label is so capacious and subjective as to be unsatisfying. But the centrality of judgement to journalism is unavoidable. As Jay Rosen has written, when a journalist tells us a story, we go 'along a route they have chosen, and there is no scandal in saying that the choice involves human judgment, which may be sound or dubious. What it can never be is absent'.[30] Judgement is what separates journalism from the regurgitation of raw information.

And there are steps that journalists can take to control for this capaciousness and subjectivity. A sincere commitment to open-mindedness is a good starting point, though every well-meaning journalist will sometimes err in their judgement. To correct for that, we need checks and balances. The judgement of journalists' sources. The judgement of their editors and colleagues. The judgement of news consumers, who can tell journalists where they've gone wrong. Again, none of these checks is infallible. Listen to them all, though, and the risk of fallibility is reduced.

In everyday parlance, the word 'judgement' can have multiple connotations: it can mean something like an opinion (*In my judgement, that was the weakest of the* Star Wars *prequels*) or something meatier (*He displayed really poor judgement letting that staff member go*). I am talking, here, more about the second type, even if the two meanings aren't totally divorced. This type of judgement implies a weighty responsibility, one that is to some extent innate but can also be refined through learning and experience.

Journalistic judgement as to what is true and important also requires ancillary attributes. One is imagination. This might sound like a concept more associated with fiction. And yet imagining how the world might be different can help us scrutinize how it *is* in reality. Many American journalists failed to imagine that Donald Trump would be elected president or that the Supreme Court might one day overturn national abortion rights – a failure of imagination that led to many poor judgement calls in how these rights were covered before the Court (stacked with Trump appointees) eventually did curtail them in 2022. Many British journalists could not conceive of Brexit happening. During Myanmar's transition, many journalists there failed to imagine the possibility of another military coup.

Judgement also requires a critical sense, the urge to constantly ask *why*. Thinking critically is a hard task that is even harder to precisely define. But it is, in my view, the key to finding the truth and reconciling that task with all the baggage that we bring to it. As Samantha Pak, a journalist based near Seattle, put it to me, it's pointless for journalists to try to remove their humanity from their work. 'We might as well have AI tell our stories', she said.

As I write, some media executives are experimenting with this idea, albeit without consistent success: AI engines can currently write competent prose but aren't reliable when it comes to distinguishing truth from fiction or writing with personality. For now, at least, judgement and critical thinking remain essentially human tasks. And, as Hamilton Nolan put it in the *Columbia Journalism Review* in 2023, even if an AI engine can produce 'a convincing simulacrum of a news story', it can never be held accountable for the judgement calls that shaped it. 'AI will always be presenting the mere appearance of transparency, never a true exploration of its decisions and motivations', Nolan wrote. 'If AI is neither accountable nor transparent, its work can never be ethically published as journalism.'[31]

***

In 2023, I spoke with Frankie de la Cretaz, a transgender journalist in the US (who uses they/them pronouns). I called them after reading their commentary on Gannett's hiring of Bryan West to cover Taylor Swift and the significance of West being a Swift fan. While critical of the hire in some respects (as we saw in the Introduction), de la Cretaz told *The New York Times* that, ultimately, West couldn't really win: 'Either he doesn't get respect from the general public because he's a fan and seen as biased', they said, 'or he doesn't get respect from the fandom itself because he's not the right kind of fan'.[32]

As we discussed Swift, de la Cretaz widened the lens, telling me that they've been told they can't cover the

LGBTQIA+ community because they are part of it, and thus biased. But de la Cretaz believes those who cover a community best are often those who 'know it intimately'. People often think that such knowledge can lead to blind spots, they said, 'but at the same time, when you know it as well as you do, sometimes you actually know where the cracks exist in a way that somebody who's outside of it might not'.

De la Cretaz also covers sport – another branch of journalism in which reporters have been discouraged from rooting for interests that they cover. But this might be changing. (West's claim that covering Swift as a fan is 'no different than being a sports journalist who's a fan of the home team' could be seen as evidence of this.) De la Cretaz recalled covering a women's basketball tournament while openly supporting one of the teams involved, without that undermining their reporting.

'For me, the things I critique the most are the things that I love', de la Cretaz said. 'Because I want the things that I love to be great.'

4
CRITICISM

Around the turn of the 20th century, an Irish bartender in Chicago named Martin J. Dooley described how newspapers 'comfort the afflicted' and 'afflict the comfortable'. (See Figure 4.1.) This idea has since become a cliché, often brandished as a noble statement of purpose. Others have echoed the idea without echoing the phrase: the newspaper baron Joseph Pulitzer (after whom the Pulitzer Prizes were named) once said that journalists, among other things, should 'oppose privileged classes and public plunderers' and 'never lack sympathy with the poor'.

Not that everyone likes the sentiment. 'There is nothing inherently wrong with being comfortable', the conservative American commentator Jonah Goldberg wrote in 2022, 'and afflicting the comfortable – *or anyone else* – without good reason is almost the textbook definition of being a jerk'.[1] Kovach and Rosenstiel, in their *Elements of Journalism*, describe the phrase 'comfort the afflicted and afflict the

Figure 4.1: Martin J. Dooley (right) drawn by E.W. Kemble

comfortable' as having unfortunate liberal overtones. Journalism's role as a 'watchdog', they argue, is 'deeper and more nuanced than the literal sense of *afflicting* or *comforting* would suggest', and 'more properly means watching over the powerful few in society to guard, on behalf of the many, against tyranny'.[2]

While I'm loathe to throw out a perfectly good cliché just because those of a certain political persuasion might not like it, the words 'afflict' and 'comfort' aren't the best that Dooley could have chosen. Reorient the phrase around the concept of power, however, and it remains a useful manifesto for journalism.

In some countries there is still a tradition of journalism that takes afflicting the comfortable quite literally. 'In each paper, there's a will to fuck over the powerful', the anonymous UK journalist told me, making clear that he thought this a good thing. 'There's a real appetite to just go after people.' (Of course, in a class-based society, there are limits to this mindset. The British media going after members of the royal family tends to be frowned upon. Well, parts of the royal family – just ask Meghan Markle.)

On the whole, mainstream US newsrooms tend to be less aggressive towards those in power. Interviews with officials, for example, are often more courteous and less tough than in the UK; it is rare to hear US interviewers ask a recalcitrant politician the same question 12 times, as the British TV journalist Jeremy Paxman famously did to the Conservative politician Michael Howard. Nonetheless, the US has its own strains of journalism that are irreverent and sharp. 'I think that the role of the journalist is always to punch up', Frankie de la Cretaz told me. 'I'm always thinking about who has power.'

Rather than afflict the comfortable, we might say that it is a journalist's job to *scrutinize the powerful*. This maxim is worth interpreting expansively; in most societies, more than Kovach and Rosenstiel's 'few' exert power, even if only a relative few have high-level political authority. 'I think of power as something diffused through the social body', Jem Bartholomew, a British journalist and sometime colleague of mine at the *Columbia Journalism Review*, told me. 'Where there is power – whether that's in a welfare office, whether that's a boss over their cleaner, or whether that's a legislative body – those are sites where power could potentially be abused.'

This maxim of scrutinizing the powerful, wherever they may be in society, is hard to flip on its head in a pithy, Dooley-esque way. Some might like to throw out the notion of journalism comforting the afflicted altogether. But others seem attached to the idea, or something resembling it. James Carey wrote about the idea of news as a 'ritual'. If it is, it need not be a comforting one – but it can be, bringing a community together to mourn a shared tragedy, for example. In 2023, the science writer Ed Yong, whose sweeping coverage of the COVID-19 pandemic in the US won him a Pulitzer Prize, wrote an op-ed considering how journalists should treat people suffering from the long-term effects of the disease. 'Contrary to the widespread notion that speaking truth to power means being antagonistic and cold', Yong wrote, 'journalists can, instead, act as a care-taking profession – one that soothes and nurtures', including by making 'people who feel invisible feel seen'.[3]

The idea of journalism providing comfort in dark times is not one that I oppose, per se. Again, though, I think that it works best if we frame it around the concept of power. If comforting the afflicted is a clunky idea, journalism, in my view, *can* usefully *empower the disempowered* – albeit, perhaps, with more caveats than apply to their duty to scrutinize the powerful.

One way journalists can empower people is, as Yong suggests, simply to share their stories, an act that can make people feel seen and bring their problems to the attention of those with the power to do something about them. 'My interest in covering poverty and the reason that I think it's so important is that those people towards the poorer end of society are typically forgotten by the media', Bartholomew, who has extensively covered poverty in the UK, said. It can feel as if 'no one wants to hear about it – the camera is focused elsewhere'. When we spoke, Britain was in the throes of a 'cost of living crisis' that was getting widespread media attention – but mostly, Bartholomew suggested, because the middle classes were feeling the pinch as well.

Journalists can also empower people by ensuring that they have access to the information that enables them to make decisions about their everyday lives and needs, either by providing that information themselves or holding other actors accountable for failing to provide it. Still, if the point of such work is to make sure that people have the information they need to make important life decisions, journalists must also respect the agency of those making the decisions – an agency that implies the ability to be held to account for them. For journalists to treat certain people as being beyond scrutiny is to condescend to them.

As we have seen, power is always relative. Even within a community that we might broadly see as disempowered within society, some members likely have more power than others. And the costs of failing to maintain a constantly critical perspective, even out of well-intentioned reflexive sympathy, can be grave, not least for disempowered people themselves.

In the 2010s, Myanmar's predominantly Muslim Rohingya population was subjected to appalling abuses of their human rights, including internment, violent assault and murder. And yet Rohingya people speaking with journalists – and their translators – occasionally exaggerated their personal tales of suffering. Their instincts for doing so were not necessarily ignoble: they may have wanted the international community to care about their very real collective plight, so that it might send more aid.[4] But as Hannah Beech, who reported on Rohingya refugees for *The New York Times*, put it in 2018, false stories devalued many other true ones, as well as buttressing military claims that what was happening was not 'ethnic cleansing, as the international community suggests, but trickery by foreign invaders'.[5]

Around the same time, in the US, news organizations were reporting on claims that Roy Moore, a Republican Senate candidate in Alabama, sexually abused teenagers as an adult. (He denied wrongdoing.) One woman told a *Washington Post* reporter that Moore had impregnated her when she was 15. After doing some digging, the paper identified discrepancies in her story; they eventually dispatched video journalists to stake out the offices of Project Veritas, a right-wing group that specialized in sting operations aimed at embarrassing the mainstream media and liberal advocacy groups. The journalists saw the woman going inside. The paper never published her story, but did publish a video of a reporter confronting her about her motives.[6]

The following year, the *Post* won a Pulitzer Prize for its coverage of Moore. The citation praised the paper for 'purposeful and relentless reporting that changed the course of a Senate race in Alabama by revealing a candidate's alleged past sexual harassment of teenage girls and subsequent efforts to undermine the journalism that exposed it'.[7]

***

Journalists in the US and elsewhere have debated other philosophies that can be seen as questioning the balance they should strike between helping people and telling them the truth. These have included the approach often known as 'solutions journalism'; the idea that the news should inspire hope; and the notion of journalistic 'impact'. These concepts are not monolithic, nor intrinsically linked. But considering them in tandem can be instructive for how we might usefully think about stretching the boundaries of journalism, and how we might not.

The Solutions Journalism Network (SJN), a US-founded group that is a leading advocate of that approach, has described it as 'a global shift in how people understand and shape the world by focusing reporting on responses to problems and what we can learn from their successes and failures',[8] rather than merely focusing on the problems. 'When news reveals what's working (or promising)', the SJN has argued, it 'elevates the tone of public discourse, making it less divisive and more constructive, allows communities to see better options, and builds agency and hope'.

If problems are a part of the world that journalists must cover, solutions to those problems are often part of it, too. Sometimes, reframing a story around potential solutions can change the way that an issue is discussed in society, with concrete, positive consequences. Road safety is one such issue. News organizations all over the world have often blamed car crashes on individual drivers or victims, but in recent years, more journalists, prompted by the World Health Organization (WHO) and other groups, have sought to incorporate structural explanations, like vehicle and road design, into their coverage. This in turn has changed how some members of society and policy makers have thought about preventing road deaths. Matts-Åke Belin, a WHO official, told me in a 2023 interview that journalists in Sweden helped pressure the government to install new safety barriers that have proven highly effective.[9]

The SJN and other advocates for solutions journalism have stressed that the point of the approach isn't to be Pollyannaish. Coverage of solutions, they say, should supplement, rather than replace, coverage of social problems. And it should be evidence-driven: if a particular solution isn't working, journalists shouldn't hide that fact.[10] Still, some of the rhetoric around solutions journalism can border on the evangelical. (One of the founders of the SJN has spoken of changing 'the moral imagination of the world'.) As I see it, journalists should be deeply humble and sceptical about proposed solutions to social problems, particularly those that have proven intractable.

And they should always interrogate *which* solutions policy makers consider 'credible' or 'achievable' and which they don't. 'Legacy newsrooms have made more efforts to include solutions in their coverage, which I think is to be welcomed. Whether they always present the full range of solutions, and not just the *politically possible* solutions, is another question', Bartholomew told me. In the modern age, 'society has been remade in huge, dramatic ways and can be remade again. But you're unlikely to read that in much solutions journalism'. The approach, in other words, can border on the technocratic, too.

Solutions to big problems, of course, can be very simple on a technical level, but hard to implement due to a lack of political will or, worse, corrupt interests strangling the political process to preserve the status quo. 'It's almost farcical how easy the solution is for a lot of the stuff that I [cover]', the anonymous UK newspaper journalist told me. Often, it boils down to 'don't do this shit'.

Solutions journalism has been namechecked as one antidote to the perceived excessive negativity of the news media. According to many critics, major news organizations have a bias towards covering things that are wrong with the world; as a result, these critics say, many news consumers feel overwhelmed and tune out.[11] As Bartholomew reported for the *Columbia Journalism Review* in 2023, a number of initiatives have popped up (including at major news organizations) that aim to tell more positive stories.[12] Some – like *Reasons to be Cheerful*, an online magazine founded by the musician David Byrne – start from the premise that excessive negativity produces a skewed, inaccurate view of the world. Others offer something more like escapism. The founder of one project described negative news as 'junk food', when everyone needs a balanced diet.

As with solutions journalism, there is merit to this. Journalists shouldn't present a gratuitously negative view of the world because doing so can distort the truth; indeed, journalists shouldn't present a view of the world that is gratuitous in *any* respect. Even in dark times, the world is full of hopeful stories that merit journalists' attention, because they're important or delightful or simply fun. There's nothing to say that such stories can't be in the public interest.

But here, too, I see caveats. First, even if journalists do promote a negative view of the world, many news consumers would appear to be drawn to it. One 2019 study found that 'all around the world, the average human is more physiologically activated by negative than by positive news stories' (even if there is 'a great deal of variation across individuals' and news producers 'should not underestimate the audience for positive news content'[13]). Other studies have suggested something similar.[14] Somewhat counterintuitively, one 2024 survey out of Austria found that many people who said they avoided the news because they found it unduly negative still consumed a lot of it.[15] Other researchers have found that self-professed news avoiders still encounter a lot of news indirectly, on social media or via family members.[16]

While we should all clearly desire a citizenry that is aware of and engaged with the news, society doesn't require its members to mainline information 24/7. Despite the financial decline of the media industry and creeping threats to press freedom, news today is extraordinarily abundant, or at least *available*, in much of the world, a reality that is itself overwhelming. People choosing to dip in and out of the news isn't necessarily a problem. I sometimes choose to tune out the news – and I'm a journalist.

Given this abundance, journalists – while powerful in their ability to shape how people think about the world, as we saw in the previous chapter – generally can't dictate which news people consume, or when or how. This has always been the case, but in the internet age, news has been radically disaggregated; many people no longer subscribe to a newspaper, with its editorially curated mix of articles, but consume individual stories from diverse sources that come their way via a web search or social media platform, steered by algorithms that often amplify the reach of angry or inflammatory content. People consume information in ways that are 'probably not as guided and purposeful' as journalists might imagine, Jack Shafer, the American media critic, told me. Instead, he argued, people read the way they might eat from a *smörgåsbord*.

In this environment, forcing a particular diet on news consumers – *Eat less junk food!* – is impossible, or close to it. The internet has also collapsed the distance between news consumers and things going on far away. As Max Fisher put it in *The New York Times* in 2022, the world today is, by many statistical measures, better off than in the past, but 'with news consumption far greater than it once was, even those who live far from crises now live in a digital world of constant, dire updates'.[17] One could argue that this is less the fault of journalists than a side effect of technological progress.

Both solutions journalism and the desire for more positive news are concerned, at least to some extent, with the notion of journalistic impact: the idea that journalists shouldn't think of their work in a vacuum but should consider how it might imprint the world around it. Journalism is often deemed valuable if it leads to some form of real-world accountability: a politician resigning, a flawed policy being changed, a family being reunited. Impact, in this sense, can guide which journalists get funding for their work, and who wins awards.

Sometimes, journalism *does* have an obvious, immediate impact. That can be gratifying. But readers of, and donors to, journalism should keep in mind that impact can be harder to measure than a president resigning in disgrace. 'Nine times out of ten, you don't immediately succeed in changing anything', the anonymous UK journalist told me of his work – but that doesn't mean that the nine stories are worth less than the tenth. 'Putting stuff on the public record is really valuable', this journalist said. 'Even if you don't immediately change everything, you can create that narrative that starts to change things.' Impact can be cumulative.

If journalists can't dictate how people consume their work, nor can they control its consequences. Plenty of worthwhile journalism has no impact at all, immediate or otherwise. Arguably, this is true now more than ever. Politicians the world over seem to have learned that the most effective response to scandal isn't to change course or resign, but to cry 'fake news!' and double down. As the British dramatist David Hare, who has explored this theme in his work, once put it, 'disgrace is no longer a real thing for politicians; they just brazen everything out'.[18]

***

Ultimately, when *solutions* journalism or *good news* journalism or *impactful* journalism is done well, these qualifiers become unnecessary – it's just *good* journalism, showcasing sound judgement as to what's true and important about the world. Rethinking journalism about car crashes to account for structural factors like vehicle and road design, for example, isn't only desirable for its potential life-saving outcomes, but because it tells a truer story as to what causes crashes than lazily blaming the driver or the victim.

The world we inhabit is the result of a chain of decisions, none of them inevitable. Journalism, as we have seen, can help inform those decisions and how people think about them. Again, though, journalists can't control those decisions – just as they cannot mandate certain solutions or make the world a happier place or impose themselves on a certain politician or process. Yoking the purpose of journalism to its outcomes thus strikes me as dicey, especially when journalism has sources of social value that *are* squarely within journalists' gift.

Journalism should be relentlessly critical. Here, I am referring to 'criticism' not as negative feedback but as a process of thought or analysis; the act of evaluating, probing or teasing out an idea. 'They wholly mistake the nature of criticism who think its business is principally to find fault', the 17th-century English poet John Dryden once wrote. 'Criticism, as it was first instituted by Aristotle, was meant as a standard of judging well.'[19] Dryden was talking about literary criticism. But his words also apply to the everyday process of thinking about the world around us.

Again, solutions journalism and good-news journalism are often critical, in this sense. And criticism should never tip over into *cynicism*, a poor cousin of the concept that, I would argue, is not a form of critical thinking at all since it involves reflexive negative assumptions. Still, it *is* a fundamental purpose of journalism to constantly ask questions of the world. A journalist's primary job is not to celebrate the routine or expected. (Safe and uneventful car journeys are not news stories, even if the road-design principles that facilitate them might be.) Even in a well-functioning society, some institution or policy could always work better than it does. It is the job of journalism to find and interrogate these failures, and to bring them to public attention. To do so is not to nit-pick or doom-monger.

Nor is it the role of journalism, in my view, to give people hope – at least not *false* hope. If an aspect of the world is bleak, journalists must show that truth unflinchingly. A news organization might choose to offset that with a newsletter dedicated to cute cat photos, but it is under no obligation to serve some set diet of happy and unhappy news, or to make people feel better about the latter. Journalists are not nutritionists or counsellors.

Critical thought should infuse every type of journalism. This does not mean that every piece of journalism must serve up explicit, deeply probing analysis. Some types of journalism – 'wire copy' produced by news agencies, for example – are useful because they quickly and economically present raw facts. Even these types of journalism, though, should be the product of a critical mind; journalists producing this content must question the veracity and relevance of the facts they are communicating and choose the best words to express them. At the opposite end of the spectrum, opinion journalism, too, should be a critical exercise – even if its intention is, ultimately, to win the reader over to a particular way of thinking.

Sometimes, a journalist might choose, quite justifiably, not to report on a problem that they have uncovered. On occasion, the stakes of such a decision might even be life or death; if disseminating information about a secret national-security matter, for example, could lead to disastrous consequences, then journalists should of course think twice. But the choice to withhold information itself calls for rigorous critical thought. A national-security scenario, for instance, requires weighing the risk and likelihood of disaster against the social benefits of disclosure, and evaluating the honesty of official entreaties to keep the information secret. As history has shown, such entreaties are not always to be trusted.

* * *

In 2024, I served as a juror for the Pulitzer Prizes, in the 'Criticism' category. I was completing this book at the time and had thus been thinking a lot about the role of criticism in journalism, in the expansive sense outlined in this chapter. But the Pulitzer entries I was tasked with judging tended to be narrower in focus. Mostly, they were examples of 'criticism' as a subgenre of journalism, one concerned with the assessment of artistic and aesthetic merit in film, TV, art, architecture, music and other cultural products.

This type of work is important: culture adds richness to all our lives and is itself a source of power (as the case of Taylor Swift illustrates). But there are fears that cultural criticism is fading. As traditional local news organizations have withered, they have cut staff whose full-time job it was to critique the local artistic scene. In early 2024, it was reported that *Pitchfork*, a beloved US music publication, would be folded into a (very different) brand under the same corporate parent, and lay off much of its staff.

The sense of loss here is not merely economic. In the past, 'people didn't just want to talk about music, they wanted to talk about it as though it was art and also about what it said about us as a society, as Americans, as a culture', the journalist Israel Daramola told my *Columbia Journalism Review* colleague Feven Merid following the *Pitchfork* cuts. 'That way of looking at music is just completely gone, even by the people who still care enough to write about it.'[20] Others have argued that the music journalists who are left increasingly pay lip service to major corporate artists with energized fan bases – not least Swift. Such coverage, Hannah Williams wrote in *The New Statesman*, is 'a disservice to journalist, audience and artist alike, a Faustian bargain that leaves us only with smooth-pored photo shoots and printed hagiographies – fools of the court competing for the attention of their queen'.[21]

At least in some corners of the media industry, deeply probing cultural criticism remains alive and well. (I had to read a lot of it while serving as a Pulitzer juror. The award ultimately went to Justin Chang, an outstanding film critic who had just moved to *The New Yorker* from the *Los Angeles Times*, another local paper that was making deep cuts at the time.) Other subgenres of journalism that engage with the world in specific, yet highly critical, ways persist, too.

Satire is one such form. If the concept of journalism has fuzzy boundaries, satire sits somewhere near the edge of them; good comedy, after all, often relies on distortion and exaggeration – hardly desirable journalistic traits. But satirists sometimes do work that is clearly journalistic, or appears to be. One good example is the US-based British comedian John Oliver, whose show has conducted hard-hitting investigative journalism even if Oliver has rejected that label. ('If you make jokes about animals, that does not make you a zoologist', he said in 2014. 'We certainly hold ourselves to a high standard and fact-check everything, but the correct term for what we do is "comedy".'[22])

There is, indeed, a long history of news products using comedy to skewer the proclivities and hypocrisies of the powerful. The press of 17th-century England served up both cartoons and scurrilous ballads (known as 'libels') that were sung and even posted in public places;[23] one 18th-century publication circumvented a ban on reporting parliamentary proceedings by dressing its work as satirical dispatches from the fictional nation of Lilliput.[24] (See Figure 4.2.) Today, some British newspapers still employ sketch-writers whose job it is to relate political news while lampooning those making it – a task of 'human analysis', as Quentin Letts, one of its practitioners, told me, that involves drilling into politicians' vanity, pomposity, failure or dullness. In Myanmar, too, satirists have tweaked those in power, sometimes using cartoons to slip a coded message past the censors.[25]

It's important to note here, of course, that satire has not always been used to look critically at the wider world – at least not in a way that any journalist should recognize. In the post-Civil War era in the US, the

Figure 4.2: 'The Plumb-pudding in danger'

James Gillray's satirical cartoon 'The Plumb-pudding in danger' shows the then-British prime minister William Pitt the Younger and Napoleon Bonaparte carving a large plum pudding in the shape of the world.

News & Observer, a newspaper in North Carolina, hired a cartoonist to draw racist depictions of Black people as a means of whipping up fear and hate – playing into a broader white-supremacist conspiracy that culminated in a municipal coup and a massacre of Black residents. As the cartoonist Matt Bors pointed out to me, cartoons can still proffer misinformation or send a message that seeks to reinforce, rather than interrogate, the status quo.

Another subgenre of journalism – one with which I am very familiar due to my work at the *Columbia Journalism Review* – is media criticism, the decidedly meta practice of some journalists turning a critical spotlight on the work of their peers. In my experience, some journalists tend to accept media criticism as a valuable check on their profession, whereas others find the idea alien, insisting that *they are not the story*. Unsurprisingly for a media critic, I see the practice as vital: journalists are themselves powerful actors, at least in shaping how citizens see the world. They also work within a powerful industry – one that may be in decline financially, but still involves mega-rich businesspeople, workplace abuses and its share of zany characters.

Indeed, media criticism is far more than just a subgenre of journalism – it is a practice that everyone in society, from top politicians on down, can engage in. This has long been the case. When early printed news hit London in the 17th century, discerning readers 'compared reports, probing for inconsistencies and gaps in logic', as the historian Jonathan Healey has written.[26] Sometimes, people criticize the media in abjectly bad faith; politicians often do so when they don't like a negative story or want to use journalists as a campaign punching bag. Journalists certainly should not pander to their critics. But the act of media criticism itself is to be celebrated, not scorned. If journalists should think critically about the world around them, then those inhabiting that world have a right, and perhaps a duty, to think critically about how journalists do that job.

We live in an age of deep concern about declining public trust in the media. This is, indeed, a big problem: people have access to more information than ever before, but also more misinformation, and many politicians – not to mention charlatans and grifters within the media industry itself – would happily lead them to the latter. This is not a problem I claim to know how to solve. But I would argue that no one *should* trust 'the media' as a whole – that category is too multitudinous to deserve it – or even any one outlet in its entirety. Encouraging consumers to assess the news they are being fed – to check it, compare it, probe it for *inconsistencies and gaps in logic* – might lead them to doubt things that are true. But the alternative – ordering them not to think about it at all – is the hallmark of tyrants, not to mention liable to backfire.

As the scholar Michael Schudson once put it, 'Everyone in a democracy is a certified media critic, which is as it should be' (even if, in his view, 'most criticism misfires'[27]). Not that media criticism is the preserve of democracies alone. During my conversation with Toe Zaw Latt, of the Myanmar news organization Mizzima, in 2024, I asked him how the country's journalists were thinking about balancing critical scrutiny of all political actors while also fighting for democracy, like many of the anti-junta forces. People in Myanmar, he replied, grew up consuming propaganda. 'They know it very well', he said. 'You can't lie to your audience. If you lose your credibility from the audience, you'll be dead.'

* * *

Martin J. Dooley, the bartender who described journalism as comforting the afflicted and afflicting the comfortable, wasn't a real person but a fictional commentator dreamed up by Finley Peter Dunne, a real-life journalist and writer of the late 19th and early 20th centuries. And when he had Dooley coin the phrase, he didn't mean it as a positive thing – he was actually mocking journalists for being busybodies. 'The newspaper does everything for us', Dooley said, sardonically (and in thick Irish American dialect that I haven't reproduced here). 'It runs the police force and the banks, commands the military, controls the legislature, baptizes the young, marries the foolish, comforts the afflicted, afflicts the comfortable, buries the dead and roasts them afterward.'

For years, Dunne used the character of Dooley to make serious points in a satirical way. 'Mr. Dooley's perspective was consistently skeptical and critical', Charles Fanning, an expert on Dunne's work, has written. 'The salutary effect of most pieces was the exposure of affectation and hypocrisy through undercutting humor and common sense.'[28] (Not that those Dunne skewered were always upset by the criticism: President Theodore Roosevelt, for one, was a fan of his work, which was reportedly read aloud in cabinet meetings.[29])

Dunne's work was also deeply rooted in the working-class Irish American community, using Dooley's voice to explore the process of immigrant assimilation into a new society, among other themes;[30] as Fanning put it, he evoked 'the most solidly realized ethnic neighborhood in nineteenth-century American literature'.[31] The idea of journalism as a reflection, or even a *creator*, of community is still very much with us today. So, too, are questions as to how much members of a community should expect journalists to do for them – even if these days, few would expect them to bury the dead or roast them afterwards.

5
COMMUNITY

Dearest gentle reader: In the smash-hit Regency costume drama *Bridgerton*, denizens of the 'Ton', London's well-heeled elite, are often united in anticipation of the latest edition of *Lady Whistledown's Society Papers*, a scandalous gossip sheet. 'Lady Whistledown' is a pseudonym – being outed as the author would spell social ruin – and yet her work ties that same society together in conversation and tears it apart in conflict, derailing friendships and even a marriage (but that's enough spoilers). Even the Queen is obsessed with it, without always appreciating the contents. 'For a community that is very ordered and very restrictive in its design to have somebody come and shake that up ... I always think of it as a Christmas globe where the snow's falling and you have a scene, but then this kind of chaos of beauty is falling', Golda Rosheuvel, who plays the Queen, has said. Whistledown 'helps the Ton shake itself up'.[1]

The sharing of information has long shaped real societies, too. The dissemination of written news helped bind the Roman empire by enabling administrative conformity, while spreading common values (among Romans, if not always those they conquered). Hundreds of years later, newspapers helped establish something approaching a national identity in revolutionary America.[2] As the United States expanded westwards, the spread of news contributed to national bonds;[3] Alexis de Tocqueville, a French aristocrat and observer of 19th-century US democracy, argued that it took newspapers to unite disparate individuals around a common purpose, particularly given America's decentralized administrative structure. ('Nothing but a newspaper can drop the same thought into a thousand minds at the same moment', he wrote.[4]) President Franklin Roosevelt's revolutionary radio addresses (his so-called 'fireside chats') helped centralize political power during the Great Depression and the Second World War.[5] The Federal Writers' Project – a publicly funded Depression-era programme that put writers to work producing guidebooks, among other literature – aimed in part to foster a sense of unity.

If the sharing of news has been credited with contributing to the formation of national identities, the same has been true of other types of identity. Writing a hundred years ago, the sociologist Robert E. Park explored the influence of newspapers serving European immigrant communities in the US, which, various editors argued, accelerated assimilation by providing the practical and cultural information immigrants needed to navigate their new communities.[6] Even earlier than that, in the 1820s, *Freedom's Journal*, the first newspaper run solely by Black Americans, launched in New York. ('We wish to plead our own cause', the editors wrote in the inaugural issue. 'Too long have others spoken for us.') In the 1950s, Black publications would identify and own a journalistic 'beat' covering the emerging civil rights movement long before most white-owned publications woke up to its significance, as Gene Roberts and Hank Klibanoff document in their book about the media of the era, *The Race Beat*.[7] During the COVID-19 pandemic that began in 2020, Black outlets more consistently centred racial disparities in medical outcomes than the mainstream press, as Cheryl Thompson-Morton, the director of the Black Media Initiative at the City University of New York, told me at the time.[8]

If the dissemination of news has always helped bind communities, however, it has long played a role in separating them, or pitting them against each other. While some editors credited immigrant newspapers in the US as engines of assimilation, Park found at least one editor who saw them as entrenching segregation instead, by isolating immigrants in foreign-language bubbles. Too often, news organs have even seeded intercommunal hate. As we saw in the last chapter, the *News & Observer* in North Carolina espoused a virulent white supremacy that had violent consequences.[9]

In the civil rights era, white-owned papers across the South were often steadfast in their support of continued segregation. In one extraordinary incident in 1956, the *Advertiser* in Montgomery, Alabama, was set to print a story claiming that civil rights leaders had agreed to end the famous bus boycott they launched to protest segregated seating. The story – which had been planted by local officials, and only made it into print as a result of 'complicity, indifference, or laziness' on the paper's part, as Roberts and Klibanoff put it – was false; there was no agreement to end the boycott. But the fact of its publication could have tricked participants into *thinking* the boycott was over. In the end, a Black reporter working in a different state learned of the story, thought it didn't sound right and called Martin Luther King, who set out around town to tell people not to believe what they would read in the *Advertiser* the next day. The boycott went on.[10]

Some white Southern editors were relatively enlightened as to the importance of the civil rights movement from the start; eventually, many white-owned papers covered it with more urgency. John Lewis, a Black activist who became a long-serving US Congressman, would later credit the movement's eventual success to the media as a whole. Without journalists exposing its message and the threats it faced, he said, the movement would have been 'like a bird without wings, a choir without a song'.[11]

And yet, the US media industry at the end of the civil-rights era remained highly unrepresentative of America. In 1968, the Kerner Commission, a group brought together by President Lyndon Johnson to analyse the causes of race riots in various cities, took the press to task for a lack of diversity, which, the commissioners suggested, had caused it to miss the roots of the unrest. (The news media had 'contributed to the black-white schism in this country', the commission found.) Decades later, despite some improvements, a lack of diversity often persists, with too many newsrooms failing to reflect the communities they supposedly serve. The fierce debate over objectivity that followed George Floyd's murder in 2020 wasn't only about the best way for journalists to find the truth, but this persistent lack of diversity too. Indeed, in many places across the globe, journalism remains a disproportionately white, middle- and upper-class pursuit.

If journalism is one way in which a society talks to and examines itself, as I have argued in this book, then journalists should not only listen to voices that reflect the full diversity of that society but include them within its ranks – so long as this diversification does not undermine the basic spirit of journalism, or the act of diversification itself. (Call it the *No Nazis in the Newsroom* rule.) This is because diversification isn't just a question of fairness and equity, but also essential to fulfilling the promise of journalism: a journalistic organization's ability to judge what is true and important, and to engage in constant critical thought, is impaired if that organization is dominated by a homogeneous group with a homogeneous way of thinking about the world.

The question of *what* journalism is for implies the question of *who* it is for. At least as an abstract concept, all journalism exists within a single *global* community; at the very least, it shouldn't shut people out. Ultimately, journalism must be available to everyone. If some people choose to reject it, that's up to them.

***

This is not to say that different outlets can't seek to serve one community above others while maintaining a wide lens. In addition to ethnic or other communities of *identity*, as we saw earlier, outlets can also usefully cater to communities of *interest*, or profession. I once wrote a profile of a French publication called *Flush*, which grew out of a blog that rated the cleanliness of public lavatories into a high-end magazine that used toilets as a way to examine big social questions (while also offering advertising space to the bathroom industry[12]). Niche publications with deep knowledge in one area can unearth important facts before their general-interest competitors, as when *Computer Weekly*, a magazine in the UK, broke open an IT scandal within the country's Post Office that would become a major national story (and inspire a dramatized miniseries).

Some media outlets have created forms of community around themselves. In the UK, it means something to be a reader of the left-leaning *Guardian*, just as it means something to be a reader of the right-leaning *Sun* – even if neither group is a monolith. (My conservative friends have sometimes called me a 'Guardianista' as an insult; I grew up reading the paper and have since contributed to its opinion pages.)

Figure 5.1: A British newsstand, August 2024

Tabloid newspapers, in particular, see themselves as 'involved in the lives of their readers – every paper sale is almost like a vote', a journalist in the UK, who has worked for tabloids and who (like the British newspaper journalist quoted earlier in this book) did not want to be identified, told me. Readers of certain tabloids sometimes phone the newsroom to vent about their views or hoping to chat, this journalist said. They feel a sense of 'kinship'.

The US does not have as vigorous a tabloid tradition as the UK, but a similar dynamic holds there, too. 'Journalism is a social connector', the media critic Jack Shafer said. 'I wager that my dad, who was a religious Fox News fan, was occupying a similar province of consciousness when he watched Fox as I am when I read *The New York Times*, and that it had great use for him in his day-to-day dealings when he wanted to talk to people about current events.'

These communities of readership or viewership – often also communities of *ideology* – can be a bad thing, especially when they mutate into partisan echo chambers. Despite its 'Fair and Balanced' slogan (which it dropped in the mid-2010s), Fox, a right-wing US network owned by the media baron Rupert Murdoch (who also owns *The Sun*), has pumped out hours of inflammatory and dishonest right-wing punditry over the years, including coverage that cast baseless doubt on the outcome of the 2020 US presidential election, in which Joe Biden beat Donald Trump and Trump groundlessly claimed fraud. Documents disclosed in a subsequent defamation lawsuit brought by a voting-technology company – a suit that Fox wound up settling for nearly US$800 million – suggested that key personalities at the network didn't believe Trump's lies, but were worried about viewers jumping ship to even further-right channels.[13]

Equally, news outlets that serve ideological communities can produce good journalism. But even if a given media landscape has many publications acting in this spirit, it is desirable that the landscape as a whole be pluralistic, ensuring that news consumers have ample opportunity to hear from outlets with different perspectives without journalism from one point of view dominating. Such journalism might be of high quality in isolation, but it is likely to offer only a limited view of the world when consumed alone.

Indeed, pluralism is desirable even in media landscapes that are less structured around ideology.

It is also vital that this pluralism extend to media ownership; in many countries, very wealthy people have built up sizeable media portfolios and used them to spread their political and corporate agendas. In an ideal world, such figures wouldn't own news outlets at all. At the very least, they should be prevented by law from controlling more than one publication per market.

In many media landscapes, which I'll call *competitive*, different outlets represent different perspectives; in others, which I'll call *consensual*, individual outlets themselves seek to be broad churches (albeit, usually, within limits). The UK newspaper market is essentially an example of the former, whereas the US newspaper market is more an example of the latter; by contrast, TV stations in the UK, with some exceptions, tend to be less overtly ideological, whereas cable news networks in the US, not least Fox, tend to be more so. (Not that this picture is without its nuances: the British journalist who has worked for tabloids told me, for example, that many, especially younger people who work for such titles, disagree with their employer's politics.)

As I see it, both types of landscape have strengths and weaknesses in practice. Competitive landscapes can give a voice to different perspectives within a so-called 'marketplace of ideas' and outlets can collectively contribute excellent journalism from a variety of starting assumptions, as long as they apply good judgement and a critical mindset. They can even hold each other to account by responding to each other's journalism. But this type of dynamic can also easily trigger a race to the bottom, overrunning the landscape with journalism that uncritically echoes competing political talking points.

Consensual landscapes, meanwhile, can lead to different perspectives being considered within a newsroom before a story is published, which can make it more rigorous. But this practice can also lead a piece of journalism to be neutered so as not to offend competing political sensibilities, melting into an exercise in triangulation and perception rather than an unsparing attempt to present the truth.

Ultimately, neither type of landscape is inherently good or bad; in both cases, the problem comes when any outlet deviates from the spirit of good judgement and critical thinking. And both types of landscapes can easily become distorted. Competitive ones fail when the marketplace of ideas is imbalanced. (In the UK newspaper industry, for instance, conservative perspectives are more powerfully represented than genuinely left-wing ones.) Consensual ones fail when those with the most power inside newsrooms call the shots in a narrow or domineering way.

The value of a competitive landscape, in particular, lives or dies by good-faith competition between news outlets with a shared interest in finding the truth, rather than toxic competition driven by bad faith or cutthroat economic motives. Sometimes, such competition can seem relatively harmless, even amusing. In the 1980s, the *Daily Star* and *The Sun* in the UK entered an increasingly ridiculous bidding war to buy a donkey out of a supposedly abusive ritual in Spain. The *Daily Star* outbid *The Sun* and taunted its rival paper with the headline 'GOTCHA!' (itself a callback to an infamous *Sun* headline from the Falklands War).

Often, though, this competition has had much darker consequences. In the late 2000s and early 2010s, it was alleged that the *News of the World*, a leading Murdoch tabloid, had for years hacked the phones of various newsworthy people, including a suspected teenage murder victim, in the hope of finding information about them. In 2011, in the face of searing opprobrium, Murdoch shut the paper down. (He launched a Sunday edition of *The Sun* in its stead.) Other tabloids have been accused of similarly invasive practices.

Not that the episode reflected a total failure of Britain's ultra-competitive print landscape. The breadth of the scandal may very well have stayed hidden had it not been for dogged reporting on the part of a rival, liberal newspaper: *The Guardian*.

* * *

The idea of 'community' in journalism is often meant in a geographical sense, particularly at the local level. Local news performs a vital function distinct from that of national, ethnic or special-interest media, keeping people informed and convening debate across a range of topics, but all rooted in a specific place. (Of course, a given outlet can serve a community that is both local *and* ethnic or special-interest.) This type of journalism, sadly, is in sharp financial decline in many places. Studies in the US[14] have suggested that when local newspapers wither, so, too, do rates of civic engagement (voting, for example) and accountability in public administration (the rooting out of waste and corruption).

In addition to informing residents and holding local power-brokers to account, journalists have long debated other roles that they might play within their community. Various thinkers have argued that at least some journalists should seek to help 'build' their community, rather than trying to stand outside it – enabling 'connection or cohesion around an idea or an experience', as Lewis Raven Wallace puts it.[15] This could involve helping members of a community to solve a specific problem or refereeing a compromise between them, by offering those with opposing viewpoints space to argue in writing or on air, or even by convening physical public meetings at which community members might hash out disputes. Kovach and Rosenstiel argue that journalism should, in part, provide a 'public forum' that channels the early US president James Madison's belief in 'the central role of compromise in democratic society'.[16]

In the most fluid conception of this role, the line distinguishing journalists from members of the community disappears. Journalists, as we have seen, are unavoidably members of the community in which they live, with their own problems, be they mundane or existential. And members of a community who might not consider themselves to be journalists can perform tasks that are clearly *journalistic*.

Darryl Holliday co-founded a civic journalism non-profit, City Bureau, in Chicago. Among other programmes, the organization has coordinated a scheme called Documenters, a 'participatory media' network that trains and pays members of a community to cover public meetings where policy decisions are made. Journalists 'are missing something if we don't see ourselves as part of a broader ecosystem of actors in a community', Holliday told me, 'whether that's the YMCA or the local library or the local healthcare provider'. (In 2024, City Bureau shared in a Pulitzer Prize for an investigation into racial bias in the Chicago police department's handling of missing persons cases, work that paired investigative journalism techniques with 'community engagement' practices, including events.)

There is much to commend this fluid conception – journalists trying to stand apart from the community that they belong to is not only impossible, but a form of self-imposed alienation that can make their journalism worse by impairing their judgement and blocking their access to important stories. As Jem Bartholomew put it to me in the British context, the risk of journalists being estranged from, or not properly representing, their communities might be that they 'miss the next Grenfell Tower disaster', a reference to the shocking 2017 fire that burned down a residential block in London, killing 72 people, many of whom were from minority backgrounds. Before the fire, the local community raised the alarm about safety issues in the block, Bartholomew said, but their warnings didn't get a lot of traction.

The US academic Jay Rosen has helped to popularize the idea of the 'citizens agenda', or the notion that members of a community should have input into what subjects journalists cover, especially when holding candidates to account at election time.[17] This can be a clarifying act, as can journalists listening to community feedback on their published work. When he worked in local news, editors sometimes told the UK journalist Patrick Daly not to worry too much about readers' comments on his stories. 'But I always found that kind of feedback helpful', Daly recalled. 'If they told you, *Well, this isn't really an issue where we are*, they would often know better than I did.'

But this kind of approach also has risks. Loud voices and special interest groups can draw disproportionate attention to their pet issues. People within a community don't always have a finely balanced collective sense of their current and future interests, and can fall into groupthink or moral panic. The majority of people in a given town, for example, might not want to hear how climate change is ravaging their local farmland because they don't think that it's a problem – or because they don't believe in climate change at all.

And, while an act of journalism might end up facilitating a compromise on a given issue, compromise should not itself be a key part of how journalists think about their role. If America's democratic institutions are designed to yield compromise, this is not the case in other countries that are no less (and sometimes more) democratic. In practice, compromise leads to proposals that split the difference between opposing viewpoints.

Such proposals might be politically expedient; they might even work. But they are not *inherently* worthy. On some issues, there is no reasonable compromise to be had – journalists simply should not split the difference between a conspiracy theorist and a person dedicated to the truth, or between a racist and an anti-racist.

Among other forms of diversity, various commentators have advocated that newsrooms be ideologically diverse, a view that, in the US context, is often accompanied by the demand that mainstream outlets add more conservative employees, given the perceived liberal bias of their staffs. Progressives might also call for newsrooms to add more left-wing voices, seeing many 'liberal' journalists as centrist sellouts, or even conservatives. Such demands can be perfectly compatible with good journalism, as we have seen. How they might best be resolved in practice probably depends on what type of media pluralism you prefer.

At time of writing, though, the conservative movement in the US is dominated by Donald Trump, many of whose supporters believe in ludicrous conspiracy theories like the supposed theft of the 2020 election. Such views hold significant, if by no means majority, appeal within society; for journalists, it is certainly vital to understand them. But asking journalists to accept people with such views as their colleagues is untenable given the unresolvable tension between good judgement, critical thought and a politics directly adversarial to those two imperatives. Newsrooms are not required to hire opponents of their core purpose in the name of diversity and open-mindedness.

In the spring of 2024, the TV network NBC News hired Ronna McDaniel – the former chair of the Republican Party, who had been complicit in spreading Trump's lies about the 2020 election – as a paid on-air commentator, in the spirit of promoting ideological diversity and reaching a greater number of conservative viewers. A succession of star anchors at the network publicly revolted against the idea, suggesting that McDaniel's past election denialism was incompatible with their truth-seeking mission. A few days later, NBC U-turned, and McDaniel was out.

***

If it's okay for journalists to help build communities in the course of their work, the problem comes when they help build barriers that fence those communities off from one another. This is true of all types of community. Journalists serving a geographic community should strive to make locals aware of the world beyond their experience, just as journalists serving an ideological community or a community of readership should open their audiences to ideas beyond their comfort zone. If they don't, journalists can become complicit in insularity, ignorance, even radicalization.

Journalists should recognize that – while intimate knowledge of their community is broadly an advantage, as Frankie de la Cretaz argued in Chapter 3 – this knowledge can lead to blind spots. Media critics often speak scornfully of 'parachute journalism', or the practice of a journalist dropping into a place (or covering a topic) that is alien to them, reporting their story, then leaving. Sometimes, this scorn is deserved; at its worst, the practice can lead to lazy journalism that misses key nuances and perpetuates stereotypes. Sometimes, though, an outsider can see the real story more clearly than an habitué. During the civil-rights era, a newspaper in Birmingham, Alabama, attacked *The New York Times* for publishing a dispatch on the 'fear and hatred' that characterized race relations in the city, calling the piece 'viciously distorted'. Not long after, the local paper used the same characterization in its own coverage.[18]

We are living through an era of globalization, one consequence of which has been that barriers between communities have grown more porous. Journalism has itself been globalized as an industry, with its international news conglomerates, globe-trotting reporters and real-time dispatches flying around the world via the internet. Threats to journalists, too, cross borders these days, with media workers who have fled repression in their homelands finding themselves followed by bad actors, from online trolls to state assassins. In March 2018, I interviewed Jamal Khashoggi, a dissident Saudi journalist who told me that he'd decided to leave his home country for his safety. ('I always pushed the envelope', he said. 'I always wanted to have more space.'[19]) A few months later, agents of the Saudi state murdered Khashoggi at the country's consulate in Istanbul. They are believed to have dismembered his body with a bone saw.

In 2022, after Russia invaded Ukraine, two independent Russian journalists reported symptoms of poisoning in Germany and Georgia, respectively. (Russia has been known to poison dissidents, though in these cases, no definitive proof was established.) In 2023, the publisher of a Russian news site exiled in Latvia was hacked with Pegasus, a powerful Israeli-made surveillance tool, while in Germany. Again, the incident was murky – though this time, the prime suspect was not Russia (which isn't known to use Pegasus) but Latvia or another European democracy.

Journalists must also respond to globalization as they judge what is true and important for the communities they serve. The same interconnected issues – globalized financial flows, climate change, deadly viruses – affect us all, regardless of where we live or who we are. Perhaps more than ever, journalists around the world are working together to tell these shared stories (and to combat the transnational threats they face), be it informally or as part of globe-spanning collaborative organizations. In 2016, one such group, the International Consortium of Investigative Journalists, famously partnered with news organizations in 80 countries to break open the Panama Papers, an explosive story based on leaked data that exposed the dubious financial affairs of the world's super-rich.

In 2018, the group gave me insider access to another investigation that it worked on, this time examining the flawed global regulation of medical devices like pacemakers and breast implants, for a behind-the-scenes piece in the *Columbia Journalism Review*. (The project grew out of an undercover investigation in the Netherlands, where a team of journalists asked regulators to approve a new 'vaginal mesh' product that had actually been made from a net used to hold mandarins at the supermarket.) I observed an operation that was impressively well-oiled, bringing together hundreds of reporters in 36 countries in pursuit of a single, devilishly complicated story that otherwise would have existed only as fragments.[20]

Global problems demand journalistic scrutiny at lower levels than the global, of course. Even the biggest stories in the world play out on the ground somewhere, sometimes in small ways but always in ways that touch people's lives. The good judgement and constant critical thinking that I see as informing the journalistic spirit should be practised, ultimately, on behalf of a community. Whatever community a journalist serves, though, they must recognize that it is just one part of a vast, interconnected whole.

The Seattle-area journalist Samantha Pak has worked for publications serving different types of community in her career. She was previously an editor at a chain of local newspapers, where, among other stories, she covered the first known death from COVID-19 on US soil, at a hospital near her home. When we spoke in 2023, Pak was writing for a publication serving her region's Asian community and also for an online magazine aimed more broadly at Asian American and

Pacific Islander audiences. Journalism is partly an act of representation, Pak said. 'But it's also opening people's eyes to people who are different from them.'

***

Myanmar is home to huge ethnic diversity – as well as persistent conflict. While ethnic 'Bamar' people make up nearly 70 per cent of the population, the country has well over a hundred other indigenous ethnic groups, with seven minorities concentrated in geographic states. Prior to its transition towards democracy in the 2010s, the military regime repressed minorities and banned news outlets that sought to serve them, including in their own languages.

Some such outlets based themselves in Myanmar's borderlands or worked from exile, however. Several of them banded together to form Burma News International (BNI), a network that still exists today and has helped to give greater visibility to the work of its member organizations. During the transition, ethnic outlets won at least tacit official approval to operate, and, I was told, greater respect from major national media that had taken a chauvinistic attitude towards them in the past. A variety of new players entered the market in Myanmar's ethnic states, without always defining themselves as 'ethnic media'. Jane Madlyn McElhone wrote in 2019 that Myanmar's ethnic media 'has undergone a metamorphosis' – albeit a 'fragile' one.[21]

This fragility was partially economic, as ethnic and other local outlets struggled to become commercially sustainable. Sometimes, they would find themselves caught up in conflict between dominant ethnic armed organizations in their home states and the national military. 'Our challenges are bigger than mainstream media because we know the context well, and we have to think about our own security and the security of our communities', Nan Paw Gay, the director of the Karen Information Center, a BNI member, said in 2017. 'If we write everything we know, it can impact on the peace process, but if we don't write everything, the public won't know what is going on.'[22]

To do journalism for an ethnic outlet in Myanmar can involve serving at least two communities at once: an ethnic one and a geographic one, given different ethnic groups' geographic concentration. It can involve representation of a given people's language and culture – and even, sometimes, preservation, helping to keep a written communal tradition alive for future generations. It always involves providing people with information, some of it life-saving. When I spoke to Nan Paw Gay, she told me that her outlet has educated people in its community on how to get around safely, including by navigating around landmines.

But the intersection of journalism and community in Myanmar has also had a much darker side, one that was laid bare during the persecution of the Rohingya population in Rakhine State during the 2010s. At the time, senior journalists and mainstream outlets were accused of parroting the military's narrative about the violence – that it was a necessarily firm response to terrorism – and of bashing coverage that illuminated human rights abuses, especially in the international press.[23] (The long history of colonialism in Myanmar only enhanced suspicion of Western media narratives.[24]) Only a few domestic outlets even used the word 'Rohingya' to describe members of that community. Others called them 'Bengali', a derogatory term used to paint Rohingya people as outsiders.[25]

BNI was caught up in these tensions:[26] the organization and its member outlets did report on the violence, but BNI did not display articles that it deemed overly sensitive or controversial on its shared website, steering clear of the word 'Bengali' but also the word 'Rohingya'. Buddhist Rakhine journalists came under intense pressure from members of their own community, Tin Tin Nyo, who is now the managing director of BNI, told me. (She didn't work there at the time.) In general, ethnic media outlets must be 'broad-minded' and 'independent', she said. 'We serve particular ethnic nationalities. But we cannot do everything that they want us to do.'

Ye Naing Moe is a journalist and teacher from Myanmar, who is himself of Rakhine ethnicity. He has taught journalists including Wa Lone and Kyaw Soe Oo, the Reuters reporters who were arrested in 2017 after reporting on atrocities in Rakhine State. (See Figure 5.2.) They remained close; not long before the arrests, Ye Naing Moe presented a ring at Wa Lone's wedding. When the pair eventually appeared in court, Ye Naing Moe testified on their behalf. Afterwards, he noticed that his neighbours started

Figure 5.2: Wa Lone (left) and Kyaw Soe Oo

Wa Lone and Kyaw Soe Oo onstage at the Committee to Protect Journalists' annual International Press Freedom Awards on 21 November 2019 in New York City.

looking at him with suspicion. At least initially, even some journalists believed that Wa Lone and Kyaw Soe Oo were traitors.

During the Rohingya crisis, Ye Naing Moe's journalism students didn't show much concern about what was going on; indeed, they often didn't seem to understand it at all. Many professional journalists at the time failed to adhere to 'the basic principles of their profession: balance, fairness, accuracy', he said. International media got in touch with Rohingya leaders and activists and wrote stories about them. Many domestic outlets did not.

'The story of Myanmar is an epic story, kind of like *Game of Thrones*', Ye Naing Moe told me.

'What I keep saying to my fellow journalists is that you will experience many different kinds of system and ages; authoritarian rule and civilian rule. What you have to remember is, whatever the system you face, you just practise independent journalism. So that after 30 years, 40 years, 50 years, when you look back at your story [you can say] *Okay. I wasn't wrong.*'

***

The 2021 coup might have been expected to reverse the metamorphosis of Myanmar's ethnic media. As we have seen, the post-coup period had brutal consequences for independent journalism as a whole. But the standing of ethnic media arguably improved in a few respects. Writing in 2022, McElhone noted that ethnic outlets, which have long operated in the borderlands under conditions of conflict between ethnic armed organizations and the military, were better prepared than their mainstream national counterparts for the coup and the fighting that followed.[27] Journalists from the former helped some of those from the latter to join them in areas outside the junta's control, and have since assisted them with their work.

Since the coup, minority groups have had a 'bigger space' within Myanmar's media, the journalist Nyein Nyein Naing told me. Many mainstream outlets 'rely on different minority group media outlets, because they are the only sources' of information in their areas, she said. Key battles in the fight against the military regime have played out in ethnic states. As the conflict has developed, news-hungry people across Myanmar and beyond have turned to ethnic outlets' coverage to stay informed, expanding those outlets' audiences beyond their home communities.

As well as blurring the boundaries separating national and ethnic media, the period since the coup has perhaps been easiest for those outlets that maintained a presence across Myanmar's physical borders during the transition towards democracy, rather than moving their operations fully back inside the country. A 2022 report by the Media Development Investment Fund, an organization that supports independent media around the world, found that these outlets 'have proven to be among the most nimble and safe due to the strong networks, resources and teams they had already established in neighbouring countries'.[28]

Myanmar, of course, is just as much a part of our globalized world as anywhere else, no matter how much the military regime might have isolated it. It, too, has a stake in the problems that increasingly touch all of us and demand global journalistic scrutiny. This is particularly true of the climate crisis; by many metrics, Myanmar is one of the most vulnerable countries to climate change anywhere on earth. But in cracking down on independent journalism and forcing its practitioners to scatter, the military regime has stymied reporting on this and the other urgent challenges that Myanmar faces.

Thin Lei Win, who now writes about the intersection of food systems and climate change from a base in Europe, told me that the coup pushed this type of story 'really far down the list of things the country needs to sort out'. She ticked off a list of pressing climate challenges facing Myanmar: intense storms in the Bay of Bengal, rising temperatures in the central dry zone, saline intrusion in the delta area that serves as Myanmar's 'rice bowl', the deforestation of mangroves, damage from mining and extraction. 'Ooft', she sighed. 'It's a big problem.'

6
BEYOND

In the summer of 2017, after graduating from Columbia University's journalism school, I interned at a website called *BuzzFeed News* in New York. This wasn't quite the heyday of the digital-news startup, but some of the trappings remained. I went to work every day in a swanky office in Manhattan, with a balcony looking out towards the skyscrapers of midtown. (See Figure 6.1.) We ate nice catered food – bagels shipped from Queens, tacos, poke – several days a week. Sometimes, there were parties and celebrity guests in the office.

At the time, *BuzzFeed News* was arguably at the height of its relevance. Months before I joined, it had provoked a fierce debate within the world of American journalism when it published an unvetted dossier of lurid allegations against Donald Trump compiled by a British ex-spy. Many critics argued that dumping unverified information onto the internet was a violation of a journalist's duty to scrutinize it

Figure 6.1: The author on the final day of his internship at *BuzzFeed News* in New York City in 2017

and sieve out untruths. Ben Smith, *BuzzFeed*'s editor, countered that the dossier was already influencing decisions at the highest levels of government and the media; withholding it from the public, he insisted, would be anti-democratic. Trump attacked *BuzzFeed* as a 'failing pile of garbage'. *BuzzFeed* slapped those words on merchandise.

While I worked there, the site also published a series of shocking stories about suspected Russian assassination campaigns on UK and US soil that went on to be a finalist for a Pulitzer Prize, as well as an explosive investigation alleging that the R&B star R. Kelly had trapped women in a 'cult'. Not that I worked on anything this exciting: I was a copy editor whose responsibilities mostly entailed checking other people's work for spelling and grammar errors. I did publish a quiz, with my then-boss Megan Paolone, that told people what punctuation mark they most resembled based on their cultural tastes and what they were like at parties.[1]

Today, *BuzzFeed News* no longer exists. (Its parent company, BuzzFeed – perhaps always better known for its quizzes, listicles and viral gimmicks than its news division – is still going at time of writing, as is *HuffPost*, a separate news site it acquired in 2021.) BuzzFeed's broader business model, yoked tightly to web traffic from Facebook and other social platforms, took a hit as these platforms became less hospitable places for third-party publishers. The news operation, never a reliable cash cow in itself, made deep staff cuts before closing for good in 2023. I left for the *Columbia Journalism Review* in the autumn of 2017. I later worked out that, if I'd stayed, I could feasibly have lost my job on any one of three or four occasions.

The site's struggles matched those of other digital journalism outlets that grew meteorically, then fizzled. While the rise and fall of this type of company was particularly dizzying, it was hardly an aberration – in recent years, news companies of all shapes and sizes all over the world have faced financial problems, often to the point of extinction. Traditional local and community newspapers have been hit especially hard as they have struggled to transition from print – which is in widespread, if by no means total, decline as a journalistic medium – to publishing online, which is harder to monetize. The US had nearly 3,000 fewer local newspapers in 2023 than it did in 2005;[2] in roughly the same period, the number of journalists employed by US newspapers declined by more than half. (As I wrote these words, in July 2024, the US news business had already shed nearly 2,400 jobs that year, by one estimate.[3]) According to an independent 2019 report commissioned by the British government and led by Dame Frances Cairncross, the UK had shed some 300 local newspapers and 6,000 full-time journalists since 2007.[4]

Journalists sometimes see their work in lofty terms: as a noble calling to make a dysfunctional world a better place. Such mythologizing has been echoed even outside the industry – not least in Hollywood, where the journalist-as-dogged-hero is a well-worn archetype. As the academic Victor Pickard has put it, the election of Trump in 2016 caused many people to see 'news institutions as the last bulwark of civil society, protecting them against everything from fake news to fascism'.[5] Depending on who you ask, journalists are crusading muckrakers who bring down presidents, or vaccinators against the rampant spread of online disinformation, or hands-on service providers in their communities. Or all of the above. Or more.

And yet, as some journalists seem to expect more from themselves, they collectively must do it with less – less money, less job security, fewer prospects for career advancement, fewer traditional outlets for their work. As I have hopefully shown in this book, society needs journalism – and an adequate number of professional *journalists* – to fulfil key informational and critical roles on its behalf. These roles are demanding enough without adding a duty to save the world.

Journalists have always needed help from those around them. At this moment, with the professional journalism industry in crisis the world over, that need strikes me as more pressing than ever. Even if many of his prescriptions for government were elitist, Walter Lippmann perhaps diagnosed the problem best when he wrote, over a hundred years ago, that 'the press is no substitute for institutions'. The news media 'is like the beam of a searchlight that moves restlessly about, bringing one episode and then another out of darkness into vision', Lippmann concluded. 'Men cannot do the work of the world in this light alone.'[6]

***

To a certain extent, journalists will always have to serve as a backstop to other institutions. 'It could be that an elderly woman can't get out of her flat on the twelfth floor because the lift's broken, and the local paper reports that and the lift gets fixed', the journalist who has worked for tabloids in the UK told me. 'People will always fall through the cracks, and journalism, in an ideal world, is a safety net for those people.' But fixing the lift, ultimately, is the responsibility of building management, not of journalists.

Journalists will always have some role to play, too, in providing people with basic, actionable information that enables them to go about their daily lives. There can be value in journalists telling people their local pharmacy's opening times – or where to go to get vaccinated against COVID-19 or even how to avoid being blown up by a landmine. But I'm not sure that this should be their primary role either. In an ideal world, the state or other actors would provide people with this basic information, freeing journalists to look more deeply and critically at the tangled mess of information that is now in the public domain and to find out things that officials would rather keep hidden. (Of course, in an ideal world, there wouldn't be COVID-19 or landmines either.)

Journalism 'used to be about giving people basic information that they couldn't get anywhere else', Joshi Herrmann, who founded Mill Media, a network of innovative local-news publications in the UK, told me. But we're now living in 'an age of information superabundance rather than information scarcity'. For Herrmann, the role of the journalist is now to guide people through that information, by 'interpreting it, contextualizing it and making sense of it'. To that end, his outlets aim to publish fewer stories than a traditional local newspaper. But those stories go deeper. Their purpose, Herrmann said, 'is to connect the dots for people – not just to paint the dots, because the dots are already painted by the online information ecosystem'.

Something similar could be said of other journalistic roles that we've considered in this book, like the idea of convening community meetings to debate a contentious issue. One objection to journalists doing this sort of thing might be that it constitutes inappropriate interference with news that they ought to be covering as detached observers. I don't agree; at least, not inherently – as I argued earlier, journalists are ultimately members of their communities, with a stake in how common problems are resolved. But so, too, are all the other actors within a community. Why should hosting a meeting to solve a common problem fall to a local journalistic organization, rather than, say, a local good-government group? Journalists might step up in the latter's absence. But justifying this as *compatible* with their job is not the same as saying that it *is* their job.

If anything, journalists seeing themselves as part of the fabric of their communities should free them up to perform their own core functions, rather than loading them with extra duties. Darryl Holliday, the co-founder of City Bureau, told me that while society does need full-time journalists who dedicate their working lives to, for example, investigating corruption, in the end, 'journalism skills are civic skills'; tools that should be accessible for everyone in society, not walled away in expensive journalism schools. If more people knew, for example, how to file a request to obtain information from the government, they might not always need a professional journalist to do so on their behalf.

Journalists also need to earn the trust of people within their communities, especially those individuals and groups who have good reason to distrust a profession that has stigmatized or simply ignored them in the past. At the same time, there are limits. Earning trust cannot come at the expense of pandering to people or telling them only what they want to hear. Nor, as we saw earlier in this book, should we expect or even want people to trust a piece of journalism unquestioningly, without engaging their own critical faculties.

Trust in the media is a big worry for many journalists right now. In many places, it is in decline, a problem abetted by unscrupulous media-bashing politicians and unchained online discourse. This worry is a legitimate one. But the reason journalists should want people to trust them is so that they believe the stories they judge to be true and important; otherwise, what's the point of being trusted at all? While hard to quantify, I've observed, in my years as a US-focused media critic, that rhetoric about winning trust too often feels like a cipher for the old problem of not wanting to upset people on different ends of the political spectrum; of not wanting to *sound* partisan. But true independence from partisan interests means telling the truth whatever it sounds like, rather than massaging it to fit some imagined, difference-splitting centre ground.

If news consumers don't owe any obligation to journalists to care about the truth, they surely at least owe it to themselves and those around them. In turn, a society owes it to its citizens to provide them with the critical – again, often *journalistic* – skills that they need to think properly about the news and engage truthfully with the world around them. Everywhere, the world needs better media literacy and journalism instruction in schools, from as young an age as possible. There is, of course, a risk that teachers or policy makers could manipulate this sort of instruction, but this is a risk inherent to many areas of education.

There is, also of course, a broader tension in the relationship between journalism and the state. Journalists often see themselves as – and sometimes *are* – adversaries to those in government. But they cannot thrive without the latter's help. This help can be passive: the bare minimum of allowing journalists to do their jobs without facing violence or imprisonment. But it can also be more active. Governments can foster a healthy atmosphere for journalism by opening themselves up to scrutiny: they can institute and comply with robust freedom of information laws, make it harder for the rich and powerful (or anyone else for that matter) to frivolously sue journalists for defamation, regulate social media giants and monopolies that distort the information ecosystem (not to mention the media advertising market, which has been eaten up by big tech companies like Facebook and Google), help to fight the rising tide of disinformation, and curb the potential harms of AI. The list goes on.

Many journalists would like to believe that they can, indeed *must*, perform the functions that I've outlined in this book independently of government, especially at a time when democracy is under attack worldwide and many governments look increasingly like unreliable partners. That's valid – and journalists, of course, should never be complicit with those in power. Like it or not, though, journalism does not exist in a political or regulatory vacuum. Even the total absence of regulation is a policy choice that shapes how journalists do their jobs.

All this would be true even if the commercial market for journalism wasn't collapsing – and the market *is* collapsing. Journalists urgently need government help with that reality, too. Journalism cannot be *for* anything if it does not exist.

***

Even in Lippmann's day, people saw the news as an essential service but baulked at paying for it. 'We have accustomed ourselves now to paying two and even three cents on weekdays, and on Sundays, for an illustrated encyclopedia and vaudeville entertainment attached, we have screwed ourselves up to paying a nickel or even a dime', he wrote. 'Nobody thinks for a moment that he ought to pay for his newspaper. He expects the fountains of truth to bubble, but he enters into no contract, legal or moral, involving any risk, cost or trouble to himself.'[7]

Similar could be said today, if not of everybody. At time of writing, some major outlets, like *The New York Times*, have built thriving businesses off the back of individual paying subscribers, offering them, if not vaudeville entertainment, then recipes and puzzles in addition to news; others, like *The Guardian*, have seen some success soliciting support from readers while keeping their online content free. Some individual journalists on platforms like Substack, an online hub for subscription newsletters, are earning decent money even with relatively few readers. Various non-profit news organizations are funding their work through donations from readers and philanthropists alike – not least at the local level.

Meanwhile, news organizations are finding more creative ways to earn money. Some are selling their journalism to Hollywood production companies to be turned into movies and TV series; others are licensing their work to AI firms that use journalistic content to train their engines, among other ends. (To vastly oversimply, these engines ingest written content to teach themselves how to write like humans.) Various news companies now engage in 'affiliate marketing', directing readers to shopping websites where they can make purchases on which the newsroom then takes a cut. In 2024, a hedge fund called Hunterbrook launched a news arm with the aim of reporting investigative stories – particularly in parts of the world 'left behind by mainstream outlets' – on which the fund can then make trades in the hope of a windfall.[8]

Such revenue models typically come with downsides, however. After *The Atlantic* cut a licensing agreement with an AI company, its technology editor warned that it may just have done a deal with 'the red guy with a pointy tail and two horns';[9] another *Atlantic* contributor warned that AI firms were planning to underpay news outlets for access to their content, then use it to out-compete them by becoming one-stop-shops for online information. The Hunterbrook model, meanwhile, raised ethical questions, with critics pointing to the conflicts of interest that might come with making investment decisions based on journalism, and even questioning whether such work might violate insider-trading laws. (Hunterbrook insisted that its news arm only does work that is in the public interest, based on information that was already in the public domain.) Even the subscription model has risks, incentivizing publications to tell readers what they wish to hear while shutting out those who can't afford to hear it.

And, taken together, inventive revenue streams aren't working at the scale required to preserve the journalism industry, even if they work for individual players. The non-profit model – often held up over the years as a hopeful alternative to for-profit journalism – is no panacea; in 2023, several leading non-profit newsrooms in the US made cuts. The same year, 22 US philanthropic organizations teamed up to pledge an initial US$500 million investment in local news. This was a significant sum. Yet one of the leaders of the initiative acknowledged that the amount in question, when split across 50 states over five years, risked being 'grossly inadequate'.[10] (The initiative planned to raise the same amount of money again from local communities.) Another said that the initiative would also push for media policy reform, noting that 'the government just has more money, period, than all of philanthropy put together'.[11]

In his book *Democracy Without Journalism?* Pickard makes a compelling case that the market-driven approach to news has failed, particularly in the US. Borrowing in part from common concepts in economics, Pickard defines news as both a 'public good' – in the sense that it has social value beyond making money, and also in the sense that it is hard to stop people from consuming it without paying for it – and a 'merit good', meaning that it is important for society regardless of whether consumers want it or not.[12] And yet, particularly in recent decades, US policy makers have typically left funding for journalism to the vicissitudes of the market. While other countries have taken less libertarian approaches, this is far from just a US problem. In her 2019 report, for example, Cairncross concluded explicitly that the market for public-interest news had failed in the UK, too, and that 'public intervention may be the only remedy'.[13]

Many democratic governments, including the UK's, already help to fund journalism, be it via subsidies to private media companies or the provision of public broadcasting or both. (In the UK, the BBC has historically been funded by a 'licence fee' levied on households that watch television.) Even in the US, there is a long history of the government supporting journalism, as Pickard attests. In the country's early days, it heavily subsidized the postal service, which was then primarily used for the delivery of newspapers. In the 1910s, voters in Los Angeles opted to found a municipal newspaper (though they cut its funding a year later in a poll with lower turnout[14]).

At some point, though, many American journalists came to see government intervention in the media business as anathema – a violation, even, of the sacred journalistic independence enshrined in the First Amendment. Compared to other wealthy democracies, the US government now spends a pittance on public media (on a per capita basis).[15] While public broadcasters do exist, a large portion of their funding comes from private sources. At time of writing, US public media outlets had themselves cut hundreds of jobs in the past year.[16]

There is also evidence, though, that the stigma around state support for news is starting to recede. National-level lawmakers have proposed, if not yet passed, a range of measures to financially support journalism, from various tax breaks for local outlets and their subscribers to a bill that would empower certain outlets to negotiate compensation from major social media companies that make money from hosting news content. Some individual states, meanwhile, have already started to implement similar policies. In 2022, California created a fellowship programme that implants early-career journalists in local newsrooms.[17] In 2024, lawmakers in New York and Illinois passed tax-credit measures. 'I was skeptical of government involvement in news', Steve Stadelman, who worked as a news presenter on local TV before winning election to the Illinois State Senate, said. But 'I think we're at a point where there are ways that this can be done carefully and thoughtfully.'[18]

The biggest fear about government funding for journalism is that it will pervert the core missions of the profession: critics of the idea ask how journalists can be expected to tell the unvarnished truth about those in power if those in power are the ones ultimately paying their salaries. This is a fair concern; public funding for journalism clearly needs to be administered in such a way that officials can't withhold it when they don't like the journalism in question. As I see it, though, every method of funding journalism is vulnerable to such conflicts. Power is not the preserve of government officials alone; private business owners have it, too, as do philanthropists. Indeed, rich people can accumulate significant power by acquiring media companies. It's a cliché to say that Rupert Murdoch has more power than many heads of state. But it's true.

If the government can censor journalism, so, too, can the market, albeit with a hidden hand rather than an iron fist. In a purely commercial system, journalism that isn't profitable can't thrive, however true or important it may otherwise be. The philanthropic model itself shapes what journalists can cover: 'Even well-meaning donors', Pickard writes, 'typically focus on certain issues while neglecting others'.[19]

And, while publicly funded media is of course vulnerable to government interference in theory, it doesn't have to be in practice. Indeed, some research suggests that government support for journalism in various countries hasn't neutered journalists' reporting on those governments.[20] In parts of Scandinavia, state subsidies have been credited with making newspapers *more* aggressive towards political parties, which previously played a bigger role in funding the press.[21]

In many countries – military dictatorships like Myanmar, for example – the hope of well-funded, truly independent public journalism is a very long way off. Even in strong democracies with robust institutional arrangements, it can be hard to totally insulate public media from official pressure (as various government efforts to lean on the BBC over the years have shown in the UK). In the US, enhanced national-level support for journalism would have to be voted through a political system that often struggles just to keep the lights on. In such political terrain, public funding for journalism might seem like a utopian ideal. Some might call it a pipe dream.

As Pickard and others have argued, though, just talking about public support for journalism – and pointing out that it has happened before, without the sky caving in – is an essential prerequisite if such funding is to come to pass. The libertarian vision of market-funded journalism is itself underpinned by a raft of assumptions and articles of faith, many of them utopian in their own way, if horribly flawed in practice.

As I noted at the beginning of this book, when I asked my interviewees the question *What is journalism for?*, one answer that I heard was 'to make money'. For Murdoch and his ilk, perhaps this is *the* answer to the question. There's nothing inherently wrong with journalism making money – indeed, things would be much easier if it reliably did. But journalism guided by the spirit that I've outlined in this book – essential, probing journalism that is squarely in the public interest – does not always turn a commercial profit;

far from it. At most, profit can only be considered a desirable side effect of journalism. It cannot be considered its *raison d'être*.

Ultimately, journalism can perhaps be thought of less as a private endeavour and more as a part of governance – not in any institutional, policy-making sense, but as one essential ingredient of a people's ability to govern itself, however that self-government might look. Being part of the concept of *governance* while serving as a critical check on the *government* is a devilish balancing act. But it is one journalists must try to pull off. It is fundamental to what they are for.

***

If envisioning a supportive role for government within journalism sounds utopian, especially in the current geopolitical climate, so might many of the other ideas that I've considered in this book. I make no apology for that – I've tried, at least in part, to answer the question of what journalism is for in an idealized sense. As I promised at the beginning, I have also tried to tread a path between pure abstraction and the circumstances that shape – and, often, limit – these ideals in the real world. Yet it's still worth clinging to them. Doing so offers journalists a guiding light, even if they can't always reach the end of the tunnel.

At the same time, even my idealized notion of journalistic purpose is not an unfettered one. If journalism doesn't exist purely to make money, nor does it exist purely to make the world a better place;

at least, not in any messianic sense. This is absolutely not an endorsement of journalistic detachment and amorality; of the idea that journalists must stand to one side and document the world's many injustices with a shrug. It is to say that, at least much of the time, enacting substantive change is out of journalists' control. Journalists do not make or implement policy. They cannot save everyone from falling through the cracks. They do not, to borrow again from Martin J. Dooley, run the police force or the banks, or command the military, or bury the dead. To judge journalists by these standards is to set them up to fail.

This is not to say that journalists *don't* routinely make the world better. But they do so in subtler ways than those of the caped crusader. Journalists can improve the world around them simply by performing their key roles – to judge what is true and to critically appraise all aspects of society – consistently and well.

This work in isolation can feel inadequate, especially in a world that treats journalists, and the whole concept of truth, with growing disdain. But if journalists don't have the power to reshape this world in their image, they do still have immense power to shape what the world knows, thinks and talks about. Even politicians and commentators who profess to hate 'the mainstream media' often define their agenda in reaction to what that media is talking about, as much as setting one themselves.

Sometimes, journalism might change the world in a more immediate and concrete way. More often, it might change the life of one person within it, by making them feel seen, heard or valued – or, conversely, shamed, attacked or belittled. None of these are small things. They are powers to be wielded responsibly.

For the most part, though, the job of journalism is more like contributing to a shared bank of knowledge and thought – a library, almost – that anyone should be able to access. Whether people do access it, and whether they believe and act on the information, is an individual or a societal decision, depending on how you define the responsibility. Either way, it is not the responsibility of journalists alone.

In many places, of course, this vision of journalism is under assault from tyrants, and journalists have found themselves having to fight back, if only by daring to continue doing their jobs. Everywhere that journalism survives, though, it remains a part of the idea of governance, however abstractly; a resource for a global public that cannot be destroyed, even if the communities that comprise it can be atomized, suppressed or forced underground.

If journalists should conceive of a community that is ultimately global in scope, so they should think of *themselves* as a global community, united in spirit if not in opportunity. Journalists in democracies can help their counterparts elsewhere, even just by bringing attention to their plight. Democratic governments can help, too – by supporting journalists in exile, sanctioning despots who silence or abuse journalists and by making the freedom of the press a foreign-policy priority. If nothing else, doing so is strategically smart. Various authoritarian countries, not least China and

Russia, are enthusiastically exporting their propaganda machines and methods of media control overseas: inspiring copycat repression, sharing content and other resources with news outlets in parts of the world they wish to influence, and seeding disinformation and anti-Western narratives on social media.

At the same time, where journalism is fighting for its life, its survival must be locally led. We can all help empower journalists to serve their critical roles, wherever they may be, but it is for journalists on the ground to define *how* they play those roles – how best to shape the idealized view of what journalism is for to their everyday reality. Much of what I have written in this book is contingent. But the core spirit of journalism that we have encountered matters everywhere.

***

Jane Madlyn McElhone and Lisa Brooten trace international interest in developing Myanmar's media to the late 1980s and early 1990s, when the political convulsions set off by mass protests against the military regime coincided with a focus on democracy and human rights as a foreign policy priority for the US and other governments.[22] As Myanmar became a cause célèbre in international democracy promotion, foreign donors – including Western governments – provided exiled media outlets with funding, training and other types of aid.

When the military regime began its transition towards democracy in the early 2010s, some, particularly newer international donors, were quick to support the process, despite many of Myanmar's journalists suspecting that the transition might not be genuine. Early on, the information ministry invited the journalism teacher Ye Naing Moe to serve on a governing body for state-owned newspapers. Officials promised that they would soon be turned into public-service media. Ye Naing Moe accepted the job on these terms, but soon quit, convinced that the authorities still intended for their official media to be mouthpieces.

Various international donors, by contrast, seemed to want to trust these promises. 'What did surprise us is that the international community provided so much support for state media before the coup' of 2021, Nan Paw Gay told McElhone that year. 'State media crippled the private media sector, there was no evidence of concrete reform, and it was always vulnerable to military takeover. Given where we're standing now, can anyone really say the investment was useful or justified?'[23] And various donors accelerated the return of exiled media into the country after 2010 by shifting funding flows inside, even if many journalists were, like Ye Naing Moe, sceptical of the regime's intentions.

At least one major outlet, Mizzima, quickly moved back to Myanmar from exile and stopped accepting donor money; according to McElhone and Brooten, its chief executive officer knew this was a risk but 'wanted to compete like everyone else in the marketplace'.[24] As the transition progressed and Myanmar's media scene expanded, many outlets developed commercial strategies to keep themselves afloat, or at least to supplement donor income, as they adapted to the promise and perils of the country's rapidly expanding internet and grappled with many of the same financial challenges faced by their counterparts worldwide. One outlet even opened a coffee shop on its roof.

The COVID-19 pandemic, however, took a sledgehammer to many of these commercial strategies; of news outlets surveyed by the international Media Development Investment Fund (MDIF) for a report early in 2021, half said that the pandemic had caused their income to decline by more than three-quarters. The day after the MDIF published its report, the military launched its coup.[25] Things would only get worse from there. Outlets that printed editions inside Myanmar could no longer do so. Advertising revenue cratered. The MDIF worked to help outlets develop sustainable funding strategies, despite the dire circumstances. Some bigger outlets with loyal readerships found a measure of success converting readers into paying members or subscribers.

Still, Myanmar's independent media once again found itself relying on donor funding to survive. After the coup, international donors, including major non-profits and foreign governments, channelled increased aid to this media. But journalists who have worked in the country told me in 2023 that those streams had since begun to be diverted towards challenges that the international donors perceived as more pressing, not least Russia's full-scale invasion of Ukraine. At the same time, the attention of the world's media drifted away from the Myanmar story.

Having to rely on donor funding has been easier for bigger news organizations that mostly publish in English than for smaller ones that publish in Myanmar's various ethnic languages.[26] Several close observers told me that donors' preferences haven't always aligned with what journalists on the ground actually want or need. And, ultimately, Myanmar's journalists would surely prefer not to rely on them at all. 'Our goal inside Myanmar was to become a self-sustaining media business', a senior media executive wrote in an MDIF report that was published in November 2022. 'We didn't want to feel like parasites.'[27]

While Myanmar's journalists grappled with numerous existential threats – and navigated the whims of the international community – many people saw their work as an essential public service, perhaps more so than ever before; the MDIF report surveyed 32 news outlets and found that their audiences had grown by an average of 128 per cent across all platforms since the coup.[28] Inside Myanmar, the regime blocked access to Facebook and to independent news sites, but many people got around the blockages using virtual private networks (VPNs). Eventually, the regime moved to block those, too, and even went so far as to perform random spot checks on citizens' phones, punishing those found to use a VPN. In 2024, Signal, a secure messaging app used by many journalists, was also reported to have been blocked.

Despite the many difficulties they faced, the vast majority of the outlets surveyed by the MDIF in 2022 pledged to continue to do journalism. And, as we saw at the beginning of this book, if the coup motivated many citizens of Myanmar to pick up arms and fight back, it motivated many others to pick up pens and cameras despite the associated hardships and risks, either by training professionally or working as citizen journalists or both. Many of these new journalists are young. Another media executive who contributed to the MDIF's 2022 report wrote that, at that point, all his outlet's remaining employees in the borderlands were in their twenties.

At the time of writing, these journalists have nothing less than the future of their country to cover. The military regime, while still in place, is reeling after a series of surprise setbacks at the hands of resistance groups. There is, at least, a measure of hope that Myanmar might have a more democratic path forward after all – even if beating the junta, a huge feat in itself, would only be a first step down this road.

When Kira Naing, the journalist we met at the beginning of this book, went into exile after the coup, she thought that it would take at least five years before she would be able to go back. Even then, she envisioned being able to return because the political situation had calmed down, not because it had been turned on its head.

When we spoke early in 2024, she was still in exile. But, at least in that moment, she was feeling more hopeful than she had. 'Whenever I interview resistance fighters – who are not [from] ethnic organized groups, but this new generation who went into the jungle after the coup – they are optimistic, because they invested their whole lives in the struggle for a better future', she said. 'Over time, I've become quite optimistic we can actually win.'

NOTES

Introduction

[1] Arlene Getz, '2023 prison census: Jailed journalist numbers near record high; Israel imprisonments spike', Committee to Protect Journalists, January 2024, https://cpj.org/reports/2024/01/2023-prison-census-jailed-journalist-numbers-near-record-high-israel-imprisonments-spike/#worst-jailers-of-journalists.

[2] Ye Mon, 'I reported on the military's abuses, and then I became a victim', *Frontier Myanmar*, 16 September 2022, https://www.frontiermyanmar.net/en/i-reported-on-the-militarys-abuses-and-then-i-became-a-victim/.

[3] Ali Fowle, '"I don't want to take a rest"', *Columbia Journalism Review*, 17 April 2023, https://www.cjr.org/analysis/myanmar-press-in-exile.php.

[4] See: Nyein Nyein, 'In Myanmar, citizen journalism is connecting news to its revolutionary roots', *The Irrawaddy*, 18 March 2024, https://www.irrawaddy.com/news/burma/in-myanmar-citizen-journalism-is-connecting-news-to-its-revolutionary-roots.html; and Thu Thu Aung, 'Dying to tell a story: The role of citizen journalists in Myanmar', Reuters Institute for the Study of Journalism, September 2023, https://reutersinstitute.politics.ox.ac.uk/sites/default/files/2024-07/RISJ%20Fellows%20Paper_ThuThu%20Aung_TT23_Final.pdf.

[5] Tommy Walker, 'Citizen journalists fight back against Myanmar military's crackdown', *Voice of America*, 15 February 2022, https://www.voanews.com/a/citizen-journalists-fight-back-against-myanmar-military-s-crackdown-/6443032.html.

[6] Lora Kelley, 'The "song of the summer" is a myth', *The Atlantic*, 12 July 2024, https://www.theatlantic.com/newsletters/archive/2024/07/the-song-of-the-summer-is-a-myth/678994/.

[7] Chris Wiegand, 'Taylor Swift is everywhere! Could I avoid her and her music for the whole month of May?', *The Guardian*, 6 June 2024, https://www.theguardian.com/music/article/2024/jun/06/

taylor-swift-is-everywhere-could-i-avoid-her-and-her-music-for-the-whole-month-of-may.

8   Alexandra Bruell and Ann-Marie Alcántara, 'Gannett wants to "save local journalism." It thinks Taylor Swift and Beyoncé can help', *Wall Street Journal*, 28 September 2023, https://www.wsj.com/business/media/taylor-swift-beyonce-reporter-applications-a2c827c0.

9   Chris Willman, 'Gannett's Taylor Swift reporter, revealed: Meet Bryan West, the first full-time Swiftie journalist', *Variety*, 6 November 2023, https://variety.com/2023/music/news/taylor-swift-reporter-usa-today-gannett-hire-1235781178/.

10 Delia Harrington, post on X, 19 November 2023, https://twitter.com/DeliaMary/status/1726293415225401646.

11 Frankie de la Cretaz and Nicole Froio, 'You have literally one job', *Out of Your League* (Substack), 22 November 2023, https://thefrankiedlc.substack.com/p/you-have-literally-one-job.

12 Sam Lansky, '2023 person of the year: Taylor Swift', *Time*, 6 December 2023, https://time.com/6342806/person-of-the-year-2023-taylor-swift/.

13 Taffy Brodesser-Akner, 'My delirious trip to the heart of Swiftiedom', *New York Times Magazine*, 12 October 2023, https://www.nytimes.com/2023/10/12/magazine/taylor-swift-eras-tour.html.

14 Hilary Hanson, 'Magazine publishes anonymous Taylor Swift review, citing potential threats from fans', *HuffPost*, 22 April 2024, https://www.huffingtonpost.co.uk/entry/magazine-publishes-anonymous-taylor-swift-tortured-poets-department-album-review_uk_662677f4e4b0167f7bf5e4cc.

15 Edward Felsenthal, 'The choice: *Time*'s editor-in-chief on why the guardians are the person of the year', *Time*, December 2018, https://time.com/person-of-the-year-2018-the-guardians-choice/.

Chapter 2

1   Mitchell Stephens, *A History of News: From the Drum to the Satellite* (Viking, 1988), p. 18.

2   Bill Kovach and Tom Rosenstiel, *The Elements of Journalism: What Newspeople Should Know and the Public Should Expect*, 4th edn (Crown, 2021), p. 14.

3   Stephens, *A History of News*, p. 45.

4   Jonathan Healey, *The Blazing World: A New History of Revolutionary England* (Bloomsbury, 2023), pp. 59–61, 202, 229, 273.

NOTES

5 Michael Schudson, *Discovering the News: A Social History of American Newspapers* (Basic Books, 1978), pp. 14–20.

6 James W. Carey, 'Technology and ideology: The case of the telegraph', in Bonnie Brennen and Hanno Hardt (eds), *The American Journalism History Reader* (Routledge, 2011), p. 217.

7 Stephens, *A History of News*, p. 231.

8 Jean K. Chalaby, 'Journalism as an Anglo-American invention: A comparison of the development of French and Anglo-American journalism, 1830s–1920s', *European Journal of Communication* 11(3) (1996), pp. 303–26.

9 Kovach and Rosenstiel, *The Elements of Journalism*, p. xii.

10 Laurence Whitehead, *Democratization: Theory and Experience* (Oxford University Press, 2002), p. 6.

11 Katrin Voltmer, 'How far can media systems travel? Applying Hallin and Mancini's comparative framework outside the Western world', in Daniel Hallin and Paolo Mancini (eds), *Comparing Media Systems Beyond the Western World* (Cambridge University Press, 2012), pp. 234–5.

12 Thomas Hanitzsch, Laura Ahva, Martin Oller Alonso, Jesus Arroyave, Liesbeth Hermans, Jan Fredrik Hovden, et al, 'Journalistic culture in a global context: A conceptual roadmap', in Thomas Hanitzsch, Folker Hanusch, Jyotika Ramaprasad and Arnold S. de Beer (eds), *Worlds of Journalism: Journalistic Cultures Around the Globe* (Columbia University Press, 2019), p. 25.

13 Thomas Hanitzsch, Tim P. Vos, Olivier Standaert, Folker Hanusch, Jan Fredrik Hovden, Liesbeth Hermans, et al, 'Role orientations: Journalists' views on their place in society', in Thomas Hanitzsch, Folker Hanusch, Jyotika Ramaprasad and Arnold S. de Beer (eds), *Worlds of Journalism: Journalistic Cultures Around the Globe* (Columbia University Press, 2019), p. 161.

14 Ibid, pp. 194–5.

15 Lisa Brooten, Jane Madlyn McElhone and Gayathry Venkiteswaran, 'Introduction: Myanmar media historically and the challenges of transition', in Lisa Brooten, Jane Madlyn McElhone and Gayathry Venkiteswaran (eds), *Myanmar Media in Transition: Legacies, Challenges and Change* (ISEAS Publishing, 2019), pp. 15–19.

16 Jane Madlyn McElhone and Gayathry Venkiteswaran, 'The changing face of print media: An interview with news veteran Thiha Saw', in Lisa Brooten, Jane Madlyn McElhone and Gayathry

Venkiteswaran (eds), *Myanmar Media in Transition: Legacies, Challenges and Change* (ISEAS Publishing, 2019), p. 132.

17 Thant Myint-U, *The Hidden History of Burma: A Crisis of Race and Capitalism* (Atlantic Books, 2020), p. 38.

18 Kyaw Phyo Tha, 'In 1988, a brief renaissance for Myanmar's journalists', *The Irrawaddy*, 6 August 2017, https://www.irrawaddy.com/from-the-archive/archive-1988-brief-renaissance-myanmars-journalists.html.

19 Nai Nai and Jane Madlyn McElhone, 'Educating a new generation of watchdogs: Interview with Ye Naing Moe, director of the Yangon and Mandalay journalism schools', in Lisa Brooten, Jane Madlyn McElhone and Gayathry Venkiteswaran (eds), *Myanmar Media in Transition: Legacies, Challenges and Change* (ISEAS Publishing, 2019), p. 202.

20 Brooten et al, 'Introduction', p. 30.

21 Jane Madlyn McElhone, 'Media assistance in Burma's reform decade', Center for International Media Assistance/National Endowment for Democracy working paper, October 2022, p. 11, https://www.cima.ned.org/wp-content/uploads/2022/10/CIMA_Burma-Working-Paper_web-150ppi.pdf.

22 Saira Asher, 'Myanmar coup: How Facebook became the "digital tea shop"', *BBC News*, 4 February 2021, https://www.bbc.co.uk/news/world-asia-55929654.

23 Reporters Without Borders, 'World Press Freedom Index', 2016 edition, https://rsf.org/en/index?year=2016.

24 John Chalmers, 'Special report: How Myanmar punished two reporters for uncovering an atrocity', *Reuters*, 3 September 2018, https://www.reuters.com/article/idUSKCN1LJ161/.

25 Richard C. Paddock, Saw Nang and Edward Wong, 'Who was most opposed to freeing 2 reporters in Myanmar? Aung San Suu Kyi', *New York Times*, 10 May 2019, https://www.nytimes.com/2019/05/10/world/asia/myanmar-reuters-aung-san-suu-kyi.html.

26 Shawn W. Crispin, 'Threats, arrests, and access denied as Myanmar backtracks on press freedom', Committee to Protect Journalists, 12 February 2018, https://cpj.org/2018/02/threats-arrests-and-access-denied-as-myanmar-backt/.

27 Alex Warofka, 'An independent assessment of the human rights impact of Facebook in Myanmar', Meta, 5 November 2018, https://about.fb.com/news/2018/11/myanmar-hria/.

NOTES

[28] Reporters Without Borders, 'Press freedom missing from Myanmar's parliamentary elections', 4 November 2020, https://rsf.org/en/press-freedom-missing-myanmar-s-parliamentary-elections.

[29] Steven Levitsky and Daniel Ziblatt, *How Democracies Die: What History Reveals About Our Future* (Penguin, 2018), p. 125.

[30] Gene Roberts and Hank Klibanoff, *The Race Beat: The Press, the Civil Rights Struggle, and the Awakening of a Nation* (Vintage Books, 2006), pp. 21–2.

[31] Ibid, p. 150.

[32] Brooten et al, 'Introduction', p. 23.

Chapter 3

[1] Thomas Hanitzsch, Tim P. Vos, Olivier Standaert, Folker Hanusch, Jan Fredrik Hovden, Liesbeth Hermans, et al, 'Role orientations: Journalists' views on their place in society', in Thomas Hanitzsch, Folker Hanusch, Jyotika Ramaprasad and Arnold S. de Beer (eds), *Worlds of Journalism: Journalistic Cultures Around the Globe* (Columbia University Press, 2019), p. 173.

[2] Bill Kovach and Tom Rosenstiel, *The Elements of Journalism: What Newspeople Should Know and the Public Should Expect*, 4th edn (Crown, 2021), p. xxvii.

[3] Ivy Lee, *Publicity: Some of the Things It Is and Is Not* (Industries Publishing Company, 1925), p. 21, https://www.loc.gov/resource/gdclccn.25006049/?sp=1&st=image&r=-1.457,-0.03,3.915,1.676,0.

[4] Kovach and Rosenstiel, *The Elements of Journalism*, pp. 44–52.

[5] Walter Lippmann, *Public Opinion* (Wilder Publications, 2010 [1922]), pp. 13–14.

[6] Ibid, pp. 174–94.

[7] Wesley Lowery, 'A reckoning over objectivity, led by black journalists', *New York Times*, 23 June 2020, https://www.nytimes.com/2020/06/23/opinion/objectivity-black-journalists-coronavirus.html.

[8] Michael Schudson, *Discovering the News: A Social History of American Newspapers* (Basic Books, 1978), p. 122.

[9] See: Wesley Lowery, 'A test of the news: Objectivity, democracy, and the American mosaic', *Columbia Journalism Review*, 25 April 2023, https://www.cjr.org/analysis/a-test-of-the-news-wesley-lowery-objectivity.php; and David Greenberg, 'The war on objectivity in American journalism', *Liberties* 2(3) (2022), https://libertiesjournal.com/articles/the-war-on-objectivity-in-american-journalism/.

10. Mathew Ingram, 'Objectivity isn't a magic wand', *Columbia Journal Review*, 25 June 2020, https://www.cjr.org/analysis/objectivity-isnt-a-magic-wand.php.
11. Walt Brown, 'The federal era III', in Bonnie Brennen and Hanno Hardt (eds), *The American Journalism History Reader* (Routledge, 2011), p. 120.
12. Jon Allsop, 'Q&A: Historian Rick Perlstein on media "bothsidesism," and why 2020 definitely isn't 1968', *Columbia Journalism Review*, 26 October 2020, https://www.cjr.org/q_and_a/rick-perlstein.php.
13. Jay Rosen, 'The view from nowhere: Questions and answers', *Press Think*, 10 November 2010, https://pressthink.org/2010/11/the-view-from-nowhere-questions-and-answers/.
14. Lewis Raven Wallace, *The View From Somewhere: Undoing the Myth of Journalistic Objectivity* (University of Chicago Press, 2019), p. 2.
15. The *Washington Post* Newspaper Guild, '*Post* Guild statement in support of Felicia Sonmez', January 2020, https://docs.google.com/document/d/1ErQ7bN352jQZ0Ka8kCzAW8CWr2zEnUIvms5BG2Kdt1E/edit.
16. Kovach and Rosenstiel, *The Elements of Journalism*, p. 112.
17. Eric Levitz, 'Millennials aren't killing "objective" news – the market is', *New York*, 30 March 2023, https://nymag.com/intelligencer/2023/03/millennials-arent-killing-objective-news-the-market-is.html.
18. Sara Fischer, 'Exclusive: *The Daily Wire* made $22 million from commerce in 2023', *Axios*, 28 May 2024, https://www.axios.com/2024/05/28/daily-wire-commerce-revenue-2023.
19. Wallace, *The View From Somewhere*, pp. 50, 102.
20. See: A.G. Sulzberger, 'Journalism's essential value', *Columbia Journalism Review*, 15 May 2023, https://www.cjr.org/special_report/ag-sulzberger-new-york-times-journalisms-essential-value-objectivity-independence.php; and Greenberg, 'The war on objectivity in American journalism'.
21. Martin Baron, *Collision of Power: Trump, Bezos, and the Washington Post* (Flatiron Books, 2023), p. 294.
22. Hanitzsch et al, 'Role orientations', p. 192.
23. Eaint Thiri Thu, 'Covering Rakhine: Journalism, conflict and identity', in Lisa Brooten, Jane Madlyn McElhone and Gayathry Venkiteswaran (eds), *Myanmar Media in Transition: Legacies, Challenges and Change* (ISEAS Publishing, 2019), pp. 229–30.

NOTES

24. Liam Scott, '"It became too dangerous for journalists to work," *Frontier Myanmar* editor says', *Voice of America*, 19 October 2022, https://www.voanews.com/a/it-became-too-dangerous-for-journalists-to-work-frontier-myanmar-editor-says-/6796391.html.
25. Thu Thu Aung, 'Dying to tell a story: the role of citizen journalists in Myanmar', Reuters Institute for the Study of Journalism, September 2023, https://reutersinstitute.politics.ox.ac.uk/sites/default/files/2024-07/RISJ%20Fellows%20Paper_ThuThu%20Aung_TT23_Final.pdf.
26. Ali Fowle, '"I don't want to take a rest"', *Columbia Journalism Review*, 17 April 2023, https://www.cjr.org/analysis/myanmar-press-in-exile.php.
27. Hein Thar, 'Rules of engagement: Armed groups and the media', *Frontier Myanmar*, 10 May 2024, https://www.frontiermyanmar.net/en/rules-of-engagement-armed-groups-and-the-media/.
28. Victor Pickard, *Democracy Without Journalism? Confronting the Misinformation Society* (Oxford University Press, 2020), p. 41.
29. Hamilton Nolan, 'Journalism is an action', *Splinter*, 26 August 2019, https://www.splinter.com/journalism-is-an-action-1837575893.
30. Jay Rosen, *What Are Journalists For?* (Yale University Press, 1999), p. 3.
31. Hamilton Nolan, 'Writing the AI rulebook', *Columbia Journalism Review*, 16 October 2023, https://www.cjr.org/business_of_news/writing-ai-rulebook-artificial-intelligence-journalism.php.
32. Madison Malone Kircher: 'A dedicated Taylor Swift reporter faces Swift criticism', *New York Times*, 8 November 2023, https://www.nytimes.com/2023/11/08/style/taylor-swift-reporter-bryan-west.html.

Chapter 4

1. Jonah Goldberg, 'Comforting the comfortable and afflicting the afflicted', *The Dispatch*, 26 August 2022, https://thedispatch.com/newsletter/gfile/comforting-the-comfortable-and-afflicting/comment-page-6/.
2. Bill Kovach and Tom Rosenstiel, *The Elements of Journalism: What Newspeople Should Know and the Public Should Expect*, 4th edn (Crown, 2021), p. 202.
3. Ed Yong, 'Reporting on long Covid taught me to be a better journalist', *New York Times*, 11 December 2023, https://www.nytimes.com/2023/12/11/opinion/long-covid-reporting-lessons.html.

4   Eaint Thiri Thu, 'Covering Rakhine: Journalism, conflict and identity', in Lisa Brooten, Jane Madlyn McElhone and Gayathry Venkiteswaran (eds), *Myanmar Media in Transition: Legacies, Challenges and Change* (ISEAS Publishing, 2019), p. 235.

5   Hannah Beech, 'The Rohingya suffer real horrors. So why are some of their stories untrue?' *New York Times*, 1 February 2018, https://www.nytimes.com/2018/02/01/world/asia/rohingya-myanmar-camps.html.

6   Shawn Boburg, Aaron C. Davis and Alice Crites, 'A woman approached *The Post* with dramatic – and false – tale about Roy Moore. She appears to be part of undercover sting operation', *Washington Post*, 27 November 2017, https://www.washingtonpost.com/investigations/a-woman-approached-the-post-with-dramatic--and-false--tale-about-roy-moore-sje-appears-to-be-part-of-undercover-sting-operation/2017/11/27/0c2e335a-cfb6-11e7-9d3a-bcbe2af58c3a_story.html.

7   Pulitzer Prizes, 'The 2018 Pulitzer Prize winner in Investigative Reporting: Staff of *The Washington Post*', May 2018, https://www.pulitzer.org/winners/staff-80.

8   Solutions Journalism Network, 'Who we are', accessed via Wayback Machine, version March 2024, https://web.archive.org/web/20240306154211/https://www.solutionsjournalism.org/who-we-are.

9   Jon Allsop, 'The WHO trains journalists to cover car crashes better. Should the US government?', *Columbia Journalism Review*, 31 January 2023, https://www.cjr.org/the_media_today/journalists_road_safety_vision_zero.php.

10   Samantha McCann, 'Solutions journalism is biased! (And other myths)', *The Whole Story* (Medium), 28 November 2016, https://thewholestory.solutionsjournalism.org/solutions-journalism-is-biased-and-other-myths-4b8f2beb69bf.

11   Amanda Ripley, 'I stopped reading the news. Is the problem me – or the product?', *Washington Post*, 8 July 2022, https://www.washingtonpost.com/opinions/2022/07/08/how-to-fix-news-media/.

12   Jem Bartholomew, 'Good news!', *Columbia Journalism Review*, 21 November 2023, https://www.cjr.org/the_media_today/good-news-network-gnn-upbeat-byrne-weis-corbley.php.

13   Stuart Soroka, Patrick Fournier and Lilach Nir, 'Cross-national evidence of a negativity bias in psychophysiological reactions to news', *Proceedings of the National Academy of Sciences* 116(38) (2019), https://www.pnas.org/doi/full/10.1073/pnas.1908369116.

14 Dylan Matthews, 'Why the news is so negative – and what we can do about it', *Vox*, 22 March 2023, https://www.vox.com/the-highlight/23596969/bad-news-negativity-bias-media.

15 Dominika Betakova, Hajo Boomgaarden, Sophie Lecheler and Svenja Schäfer, 'I do not (want to) know! The relationship between intentional news avoidance and low news consumption', *Mass Communication and Society*, 2 February 2024, https://www.tandfonline.com/doi/full/10.1080/15205436.2024.2304759.

16 Josh Hersh, 'The least important election of a lifetime', *Columbia Journalism Review*, 10 June 2024, https://www.cjr.org/covering_the_election/least-important-election-fatigue-apathy-trump-biden-favreau-burnham.php.

17 Max Fisher, 'Is the world really falling apart, or does it just feel that way?', *New York Times*, 12 July 2022, https://www.nytimes.com/2022/07/12/world/interpreter-world-falling-apart.html.

18 Ginny Dougary, 'Death of disgrace: David Hare on politicians who brazen it out', *Sydney Morning Herald*, 13 November 2020, https://www.smh.com.au/culture/tv-and-radio/death-of-disgrace-david-hare-on-politicians-who-brazen-it-out-20201109-p56ctx.html.

19 John Dryden, 'The author's apology for heroic poetry, and poetic licence', in Walter Scott (ed), *The Works of John Dryden, Volume 5*, https://www.gutenberg.org/files/16208/16208-h/16208-h.htm.

20 Feven Merid, 'Q&A: Israel Daramola on the challenges facing music journalism', *Columbia Journalism Review*, 14 February 2024, https://www.cjr.org/the_media_today/israel-daramola-interview-decline-challenges-music-press-journalism.php.

21 Hannah Williams, 'Taylor Swift's hollow empowerment narrative', *New Statesman*, 22 December 2023, https://www.newstatesman.com/culture/music/2023/12/taylor-swifts-hollow-empowerment-narrative.

22 David Carr, 'John Oliver's complicated fun connects for HBO', *New York Times*, 16 November 2014, https://www.nytimes.com/2014/11/17/business/media/john-olivers-complicated-fun-connects-for-hbo.html.

23 Jonathan Healey, *The Blazing World: A New History of Revolutionary England* (Bloomsbury, 2023), p. 61.

24 Martin Conboy, *Journalism, A Critical History* (Sage, 2004), pp. 76–7.

25. Lisa Brooten, Jane Madlyn McElhone and Gayathry Venkiteswaran, 'Introduction: Myanmar media historically and the challenges of transition', in Lisa Brooten, Jane Madlyn McElhone and Gayathry Venkiteswaran (eds), *Myanmar Media in Transition: Legacies, Challenges and Change* (ISEAS Publishing, 2019), p. 19.
26. Healey, *The Blazing World*, p. 60.
27. Michael Schudson, *The Power of News* (Harvard University Press, 1995), p. 3.
28. Charles Fanning, 'Finley Peter Dunne (1867–1936)', in Paul Lauter (ed), *The Heath Anthology of American Literature*, 5th edn, https://college.cengage.com/english/lauter/heath/4e/students/author_pages/late_nineteenth/dunne_fi.html
29. David Shedden, 'Today in media history: Mr. Dooley: "The job of the newspaper is to comfort the afflicted and afflict the comfortable"', Poynter, 7 October 2014, https://www.poynter.org/reporting-editing/2014/today-in-media-history-mr-dooley-the-job-of-the-newspaper-is-to-comfort-the-afflicted-and-afflict-the-comfortable/.
30. Fanning, *Finley Peter Dunne and Mr. Dooley: The Chicago Years* (University Press of Kentucky, 1978), p. ix.
31. Fanning, 'Finley Peter Dunne (1867–1936)'.

Chapter 5

1. Adam Rathe, '*Bridgerton*'s Queen Charlotte on what unmasking Lady Whistledown means for the Ton', *Town and Country*, 22 June 2024, https://www.townandcountrymag.com/leisure/arts-and-culture/a61128184/bridgerton-queen-charlotte-golda-roushevel-interview-season-3/.
2. Mitchell Stephens, *A History of News: From the Drum to the Satellite* (Viking, 1988), pp. 67, 190.
3. Bonnie Brennen and Hanno Hardt, 'Introduction to part three', in Bonnie Brennen and Hanno Hardt (eds), *The American Journalism History Reader* (Routledge, 2011), p. 144.
4. Alexis de Tocqueville, *Democracy in America* (Wordsworth Editions, 1998 [1840]), pp. 220–3.
5. Stephens, *A History of News*, p. 279.
6. Robert E. Park, 'The immigrant press and assimilation', in Bonnie Brennen and Hanno Hardt (eds), *The American Journalism History Reader* (Routledge, 2011), pp. 172–3.
7. Gene Roberts and Hank Klibanoff, *The Race Beat: The Press, the Civil Rights Struggle, and the Awakening of a Nation* (Vintage Books, 2006), pp. 13, 75–6.

NOTES

8 Jon Allsop, 'The everything virus: Two years of journalists scrambling to make sense of an ever-changing pandemic', *Columbia Journalism Review*, 8 June 2022, https://pandemic.cjr.org/.

9 Alexandria Neason, 'On atonement: News outlets have apologized for past racism. That should only be the start', *Columbia Journalism Review*, 28 January 2021, https://www.cjr.org/special_report/apologies-news-racism-atonement.php.

10 Roberts and Klibanoff, *The Race Beat*, p. 127.

11 Ibid, p. 407.

12 Jon Allsop, 'In France, a new magazine uses toilets to look at the world', *Columbia Journalism Review*, 11 January 2019, https://www.cjr.org/analysis/in-france-a-new-magazine-uses-toilets-to-look-at-the-world.php.

13 Jeremy W. Peters and Katie Robertson, 'Fox stars privately expressed disbelief about election fraud claims. "Crazy stuff"', *New York Times*, 16 February 2023, https://www.nytimes.com/2023/02/16/business/media/fox-dominion-lawsuit.html.

14 Victor Pickard, *Democracy Without Journalism? Confronting the Misinformation Society* (Oxford University Press, 2020), pp. 99–101.

15 Lewis Raven Wallace, *The View From Somewhere: Undoing the Myth of Journalistic Objectivity* (University of Chicago Press, 2019), p. 205.

16 Bill Kovach and Tom Rosenstiel, *The Elements of Journalism: What Newspeople Should Know and the Public Should Expect*, 4th edn (Crown, 2021), p. 247.

17 Jay Rosen, 'Key steps in the citizens agenda style of campaign coverage', *Press Think*, 12 June 2019, https://pressthink.org/2019/06/key-steps-in-the-citizens-agenda-style-of-campaign-coverage/.

18 Roberts and Klibanoff, *The Race Beat*, pp. 232–3, 249.

19 Jon Allsop, 'Jamal Khashoggi on press freedom in Saudi Arabia', *Columbia Journalism Review*, 8 October 2018, https://www.cjr.org/analysis/jamal-khashoggi-missing-saudi-arabia.php.

20 Jon Allsop, 'Under the skin of ICIJ's Implant Files', *Columbia Journalism Review*, 26 November 2018, https://www.cjr.org/special_report/behind_the_scenes_icij_implant_files.php.

21 Jane Madlyn McElhone, 'The metamorphosis of media in Myanmar's ethnic states', in Lisa Brooten, Jane Madlyn McElhone and Gayathry Venkiteswaran (eds), *Myanmar Media in Transition: Legacies, Challenges and Change* (ISEAS Publishing, 2019), p. 213.

22 Ibid, pp. 220–1.

23 See: Lisa Brooten, Jane Madlyn McElhone and Gayathry Venkiteswaran, 'Introduction: Myanmar media historically and the challenges of transition', in Lisa Brooten, Jane Madlyn McElhone and Gayathry Venkiteswaran (eds), *Myanmar Media in Transition: Legacies, Challenges and Change* (ISEAS Publishing, 2019), pp. 41–2; and Joshua Carroll, 'In Myanmar, journalists have sided with the military against the Rohingya', *Columbia Journalism Review*, 20 March 2018, https://www.cjr.org/watchdog/myanmar-rohingya.php.

24 E. Tammy Kim, 'Myanmar's other reporters', *Columbia Journalism Review*, 13 August 2019, https://www.cjr.org/special_report/myanmars-other-reporters.php.

25 Lawi Weng, 'Media in Myanmar: Laws, military and the public', in Lisa Brooten, Jane Madlyn McElhone and Gayathry Venkiteswaran (eds), *Myanmar Media in Transition: Legacies, Challenges and Change* (ISEAS Publishing, 2019), p. 241.

26 McElhone, 'The metamorphosis of media in Myanmar's ethnic states', pp. 210–1.

27 Jane Madlyn McElhone, 'Media assistance in Burma's reform decade', Center for International Media Assistance/National Endowment for Democracy working paper, October 2022, p. 8, https://www.cima.ned.org/wp-content/uploads/2022/10/CIMA_Burma-Working-Paper_web-150ppi.pdf.

28 Jane Madlyn McElhone, 'The business of independent media in post-coup Myanmar', Media Development Investment Fund report, 4 November 2022, https://www.mdif.org/news/the-business-of-independent-media-in-post-coup-myanmar/.

Chapter 6

1 Megan Paolone and Jon Allsop, 'Which punctuation mark are you?', *BuzzFeed*, 30 July 2017, https://www.buzzfeed.com/meganp25/en-dashes-are-jerks.

2 Penelope Muse Abernathy, 'The state of local news: The 2023 report', Local News Initiative at Northwestern University's Medill School, 16 November 2023, https://localnewsinitiative.northwestern.edu/projects/state-of-local-news/2023/report/.

3 Challenger, Gray and Christmas, Inc., 'The Challenger report: Job cuts tumble in June 2024, led by consumer manufacturing; second-highest hiring of the year', 3 July 2024, https://www.challengergray.com/blog/job-cuts-tumble-in-june-led-by-consumer-manufacturing-second-highest-hiring-of-the-year/.

NOTES

4   Frances Cairncross, *The Cairncross Review: A Sustainable Future for Journalism* (UK government, 2019), pp. 6, 27, https://assets.publishing.service.gov.uk/media/5c6bfcd4e5274a72b933311d/021919_DCMS_Cairncross_Review_.pdf.

5   Victor Pickard, *Democracy Without Journalism? Confronting the Misinformation Society* (Oxford University Press, 2020), p. 5.

6   Walter Lippmann, *Public Opinion* (Wilder Publications, 2010 [1922]), p. 197.

7   Ibid, p. 175.

8   Clare Malone, 'Is Hunterbrook Media a news outlet or a hedge fund?', *New Yorker*, 2 May 2024, https://www.newyorker.com/news/annals-of-communications/is-hunterbrook-media-a-news-outlet-or-a-hedge-fund.

9   Damon Beres, 'A devil's bargain with OpenAI', *The Atlantic*, 29 May 2024, https://www.theatlantic.com/technology/archive/2024/05/a-devils-bargain-with-openai/678537/.

10   John Palfrey, 'A billion-dollar bet on local news', *The Atlantic*, 2 November 2023, https://www.theatlantic.com/ideas/archive/2023/11/press-forward-macarthur-foundation-local-news/675847/.

11   Sophie Culpepper, '"Journalism moves fast ... philanthropy moves slow." Press Forward's director wants to bring them together', *Nieman Lab*, 20 May 2024, https://www.niemanlab.org/2024/05/journalism-moves-fast-philanthropy-moves-slow-press-forwards-director-wants-to-bring-them-together/.

12   Pickard, *Democracy Without Journalism?*, pp. 63–4.

13   Cairncross et al., *The Cairncross Review*, p. 22.

14   Pickard, *Democracy Without Journalism?*, pp. 16–25.

15   Ibid, pp. 137–8.

16   Austin Fuller, 'Growing costs, falling sponsorship fuel wave of layoffs in pubmedia', *Current*, 17 June 2024, https://current.org/2024/06/growing-costs-falling-sponsorship-fuel-wave-of-layoffs-in-pubmedia/.

17   Christa Scharfenberg, 'Predictions for journalism, 2024: More public funding for local news', *Nieman Lab*, December 2023, https://www.niemanlab.org/2023/12/more-public-funding-for-local-news/.

18   Alex Abbeduto, 'Panel of experts suggest legislative measures to reverse journalism decline', *Capitol News Illinois*, 26 January 2024, https://capitolnewsillinois.com/NEWS/panel-of-experts-suggest-legislative-measures-to-reverse-journalism-decline.

19   Pickard, *Democracy Without Journalism?*, p. 97.

[20] Ibid, p. 159.
[21] Bree Nordenson, 'The Uncle Sam solution', *Columbia Journalism Review*, 27 September 2007, https://www.cjr.org/feature/the_uncle_sam_solution.php.
[22] Jane Madlyn McElhone and Lisa Brooten, 'Whispered support: Two decades of international aid for independent journalism and free expression', in Lisa Brooten, Jane Madlyn McElhone and Gayathry Venkiteswaran (eds), *Myanmar Media in Transition: Legacies, Challenges and Change* (ISEAS Publishing, 2019), pp. 104–5.
[23] McElhone, 'Media assistance in Burma's reform decade', Center for International Media Assistance/National Endowment for Democracy working paper, October 2022, p. 3, https://www.cima.ned.org/wp-content/uploads/2022/10/CIMA_Burma-Working-Paper_web-150ppi.pdf.
[24] McElhone and Brooten, 'Whispered support', p. 118.
[25] Jane Madlyn McElhone, 'The business of independent media in post-coup Myanmar', Media Development Investment Fund report, 4 November 2022, https://www.mdif.org/news/the-business-of-independent-media-in-post-coup-myanmar/.
[26] Laure Siegel, 'In Myanmar, journalists raise media voices against the bloody coup', International Press Institute, 15 February 2023, https://ipi.media/myanmar-journalists-raise-voices/.
[27] McElhone, 'The business of independent media in post-coup Myanmar'.
[28] Ibid.

FURTHER READING

On journalism and history
Bonnie Brennen and Hanno Hardt (eds), *The American Journalism History Reader* (Routledge, 2011).

Alexandria Neason, 'On atonement', *Columbia Journalism Review*, 28 January 2021. https://www.cjr.org/special_report/apologies-news-racism-atonement.php.

Gene Roberts and Hank Klibanoff, *The Race Beat: The Press, the Civil Rights Struggle, and the Awakening of a Nation* (Vintage Books, 2006).

Mitchell Stephens, *A History of News: From the Drum to the Satellite* (Viking, 1988).

On journalists and how they see their work
Thomas Hanitzsch, Folker Hanusch, Jyotika Ramaprasad and Arnold S. de Beer (eds), *Worlds of Journalism: Journalistic Cultures Around the Globe* (Columbia University Press, 2019).

Darryl Holliday, 'What journalism can learn from mutual aid', *Columbia Journalism Review*, 19 November 2020. https://www.cjr.org/special_report/the-power-of-community-journalism.php.

Bill Kovach and Tom Rosenstiel, *The Elements of Journalism: What Newspeople Should Know and the Public Should Expect*, 4th edn (Crown, 2021).

Janet Malcolm, *The Journalist and the Murderer* (Granta Books, 2018 [1990]).

Jay Rosen, *What Are Journalists For?* (Yale University Press, 1999).

Margaret Sullivan, *Newsroom Confidential: Lessons (and Worries) From an Ink-Stained Life* (St. Martin's Press, 2022).

On journalism and objectivity

David Greenberg, 'The war on objectivity in American journalism', *Liberties* 2(3) (2022). https://libertiesjournal.com/articles/the-war-on-objectivity-in-american-journalism/.

Walter Lippmann, *Public Opinion* (Wilder Publications, 2010 [1922]).

Wesley Lowery, 'A test of the news: Objectivity, democracy, and the American mosaic', *Columbia Journalism Review*, 25 April 2023. https://www.cjr.org/analysis/a-test-of-the-news-wesley-lowery-objectivity.php.

Lewis Raven Wallace, *The View From Somewhere: Undoing the Myth of Journalistic Objectivity* (University of Chicago Press, 2019).

Michael Schudson, *Discovering the News: A Social History of American Newspapers* (Basic Books, 1978).

On journalism and Myanmar

Lisa Brooten, Jane Madlyn McElhone and Gayathry Venkiteswaran (eds), *Myanmar Media in Transition: Legacies, Challenges and Change* (ISEAS Publishing, 2019).

Ali Fowle, '"I don't want to take a rest": Reconnecting with Myanmar's press', *Columbia Journalism Review*, 17 April 2023. https://www.cjr.org/analysis/myanmar-press-in-exile.php.

E. Tammy Kim, 'Myanmar's other reporters', *Columbia Journalism Review*, 13 August 2019. https://www.cjr.org/special_report/myanmars-other-reporters.php.

Thant Myint-U, *The Hidden History of Burma: A Crisis of Race and Capitalism* (Atlantic Books, 2020).

On journalism and public policy

Victor Pickard, *Democracy Without Journalism? Confronting the Misinformation Society* (Oxford University Press, 2010).

On journalism and Taylor Swift

Taffy Brodesser-Akner, 'My delirious trip to the heart of Swiftiedom', *New York Times Magazine*, 12 October 2023. https://www.nytimes.com/2023/10/12/magazine/taylor-swift-eras-tour.html.

Hannah Williams, 'Taylor Swift's hollow empowerment narrative', *New Statesman*, 22 December 2023. https://www.newstatesman.com/culture/music/2023/12/taylor-swifts-hollow-empowerment-narrative.

Other useful resources

For coverage of the US media industry and its internal debates, the *Columbia Journalism Review* (where I work) and Nieman Lab are good websites to follow. (At time of writing, both have useful email newsletters – though given that I oversee the *Columbia Journalism Review*'s,

I would say that.) *Press Gazette* performs a similar function covering the media business in the UK. Podcasts including the BBC *Media Show*, *Prospect*'s *Media Confidential*, WNYC's *On the Media*, and *Longform* are worth a listen for insights on how the media works, and journalism as a craft. For English-language news about Myanmar, *Frontier Myanmar* and *Myanmar Now* are good resources that are also accessible to outsiders lacking prior knowledge of the country. The Committee to Protect Journalists and Reporters Without Borders provide invaluable tracking of press freedom issues globally, both in terms of individual incidents and broad statistical overviews.

INDEX

References to figures are in *italics*.

A
Advertiser (Alabama) 95
advocacy journalism 23, 57–61
affiliate marketing 128
Agence France-Presse 37
'alternative facts' 43–6, 53
artificial intelligence (AI) 25–6, 66–7, 128
Associated Press 53
The Atlantic 7–8, 128
Aung San Suu Kyi 1–2, 33–4, *34*, 35
Aye Chan Naing 7, 31–2, 33

B
balance 46, 52
Baron, Marty 54, 58
Bartholomew, Jem 71–2, 73, 77, 78, 104
BBC 130, 133
Beech, Hannah 74
Belin, Matts-Åke 76
bias *see* partisanship
Bors, Matt 87
Bridgerton 92
Brodesser-Akner, Taffy 12
Brooten, Lisa 32, 137
Bryant, Kobe 54
Burma News International (BNI) 111, 113
BuzzFeed 120

BuzzFeed News 118–20, *119*
Byrne, David 78

C
Cairncross, Dame Frances 121, 130
campaigning journalism 23, 57–61
The Capital Gazette 13
Carey, James 72
cartoons 86–7, *87*
celebrity journalism 7–12, 67
censorship 30–2, 132
Chalaby, Jean K. 25
Chang, Justin 85
China 5, 136–7
citizen journalists 7, 62–3
citizens agenda 105–6
City Bureau (Chicago non-profit) 103
civic journalism 103–6, 124–5
civil-rights era 39, 94–6, 108
climate change 10, 116–17
CNN 38, 44
coffeehouses 22, *22*
Columbia Journalism Review 19, 50, 59, 67, 78, 85, 110
competitive media landscapes 100–2
Computer Weekly 97

consensual media landscapes 100–1
conspiracy theories 106–7
Conway, Kellyanne 43
COVID-19 pandemic 72, 94, 110, 139
critical thinking 82–3
cultural criticism 7–12, 67, 82, 84–9
cynicism 82

D

Daily Star 101–2
The Daily Wire 56
Daly, Patrick 105
Daramola, Israel 85
de la Cretaz, Frankie 10–11, 67–8, 71
democracy, relationship with 26–42
Democratic Voice of Burma (DVB) 31–2, 33
Dickens, Charles 25
digital transition 118–21
diversification of newsrooms 95–7, 106–7
donor funding 40, 137, 138, 139–40
Dooley, Martin J. 69, 70, 90–1
Dryden, John 82
Dunne, Finley Peter 90–1

E

empowerment of people 72–4
English civil wars 14, 23
ethnic media 111–17
exiled journalists 2–4, 5, 6, 27, 31–3, 108–9, 141–2

F

Facebook 32, 33, 35–6, 120, 140
'fake news' 14, 37

Fanning, Charles 90–1
Federal Writers' Project 93
Fisher, Max 80
Floyd, George 37–8, 49–50, 96
'fourth estate' 32
Fox 98–9
Freedom's Journal 94
Froio, Nicole 10–11
Frontier Myanmar 59, 60, 61
funding of news organizations 56, 127–34, 139

G

Gannett 7–11, 67
Gillray, James 87
Global South 28
globalization 108–10
Goldberg, Jonah 69
good-news journalism 77–80, 81, 82–3
government support 126–7, 136
Grenfell Tower disaster 104
The Guardian 8, 97, 102, 127
Guihard, Paul 37
Gutenberg, Johannes 22

H

Hare, David 81
Harry's 56
Healey, Jonathan 88
Herrmann, Joshi 123
historical development of journalism 21–5
Holliday, Darryl 104, 124
Hopi people 21
Howard, Michael 71
Htusan, Esther 33, 35
HuffPost 120
humility 77
Hunterbrook (hedge fund) 128, 128–9

INDEX

I
ideological communities 97–9
impact 80–1
impartiality *see* objectivity
Ingram, Mathew 50
inoffensiveness 52–4
International Consortium of Investigative Journalists 109–10
International Press Freedom Awards *114*
internet, impact on news consumption 79–80, 88–9
investigative journalism 19, 104, 109–10, 119–20, 128

J
Jimenez, Omar 38
Johnson, Lyndon 95
journalism, definition and use of term 15–16, 21–2, 24
journalistic judgement 64–7

K
Kean, Thomas 59
Kelly, R. 120
Kerner Commission 95–6
Khashoggi, Jamal 108–9
Khit Thit 59
King, Martin Luther 95
Kira Naing 1–4, 141–2
Klibanoff, Hank 94, 95
knowledge building 136
Kovach, Bill 22, 26, 44, 45, 55–6, 69–70, 71, 103
Kyaw Soe Oo 13, 34–5, 113–14, *114*

L
Lansky, Sam 11
Lee, Ivy 45
Letts, Quentin 86

Levitsky, Steven 37
Levitz, Eric 56
Lewis, John 95
LGBTQIA+ 53, 56, 57–8, 67–8
Lippmann, Walter 46–9, 47, 122, 127
local news 102–3, 105, 121, 122–3, 129
Los Angeles Times 85
Lovejoy, Elijah 37, *38*
Lowery, Wesley 48–9, 49

M
Madison, James 103
McDaniel, Ronna 107
McElhone, Jane Madlyn 32, 111, 115, 137, 138
media criticism 87–9
Media Development Investment Fund (MDIF) 116, 139, 140–1
Merid, Feven 85
Milton, John 23
Mindon, king of Myanmar 29–30
minority group media outlets 111–17
Mizzima 138
Moore, Roy 74–5
moral clarity 55–6
Murdoch, Rupert 99, 102, 132, 133
music journalism 7–12, 13, 84–5
Myanmar 1–7, *3*, 13, 29–36, *34*, 40, 59–61, 62, 66, 74, 86, 89, 111–17, 137–42

N
Nagel, Thomas 53
Nan Paw Gay 112, 138
national identity 93

national-security matters 83–4
NBC News 107
Ne Win 30
Nedham, Marchamont 23
negative news 77–80, 82–3
The New Statesman 85
New York Magazine 56
The New York Times 12, 16, 35, 51, 52, 67, 74, 80, 108, 127
The New Yorker 85
Newfield, Jack 52
News & Observer (North Carolina) 87
News of the World 102
newspaper closures 103, 120–1
Nolan, Hamilton 63, 67
non-profit newsrooms 129
Nyein Nyein Naing 31, 115

O

Obama, Barack 34
objectivity 24, 46–51, 52–5
Oliver, John 86
opinion journalism 64, 83

P

Pak, Samantha 66, 110–11
Panama Papers 109
Paolone, Megan 120
'parachute journalism' 107–8
Park, Robert E. 93–4, 94
partisanship 6, 9–10, 23, 56–61, 63–4, 67–8, 99
Paste 13
Paxman, Jeremy 71
Perlstein, Rick 51
persecution of journalists 2–5, 13, 27, 33–4, 37–8, 38, 108–9, 113–14, 136–7
see also censorship

Pickard, Victor 121, 129–30, 132
Pitchfork 84–5
pluralism 99–100
political journalism 52, 64, 66, 71–2, 74–5, 81
political sketch-writing 86
positive news 77–80, 81, 82–3
power, scrutiny of 71–2
profit motive 133–4
Pu Tuidim 5
public broadcasters 130–1
public funding and support 129–34
public trust 88–9, 125
Pulitzer, Joseph 69
Pulitzer Prizes 33, 72, 83, 85, 104, 120

R

race and racism 37–9, 38, 49, 52, 53, 57, 86–7, 94–6, 108
readers' comments 105
Reporters Without Borders 33, 36
Reuters 13, 31, 34–5, 113
revenue models 56, 127–9, 139
Roberts, Gene 94, 95
Rohingya crisis 34–6, 59, 74, 112–14
Roman empire 21, 93
Roosevelt, Franklin 93
Roosevelt, Theodore 90
Rosen, Jay 53, 65, 105
Rosenstiel, Tom 22, 26, 44, 45, 55–6, 69–70, 71, 103
Rosheuvel, Golda 92
Royal Society 23–4
Russia 27, 109, 119–20, 136–7

S

satire 85–7, 87, 90
Schudson, Michael 49, 89

INDEX

Sedition Act of 1798 (US) 36–7
Shafer, Jack 15, 79, 98–9
Signal (messaging app) 140
Simon, David 62
slavery 16, 33, 37, *38*
Smith, Ben 119
solutions journalism 75–7, 80, 81
Solutions Journalism Network (SJN) 75–6, 77
Sonmez, Felicia 54
Spicer, Sean 43
sports journalism 68
Stadelman, Steve 131
Stephens, Mitchell 21, 23, 24
Stewart, Potter 16
Stromae 16
subjectivity *see* objectivity; partisanship
Substack 10–11, 128
The Sun 97, 99, 101–2, *102*
Swift, Taylor 7–12, *9*, 13, 67, 85

T

tabloid newspapers 98, *98*, 101–2
TF1 (TV channel) 16
Thein Sein 32
Thin Lei Win 31, 40, 60, 116–17
Thompson-Morton, Cheryl 94
Time 11, 13
Tin Tin Nyo 113
Tirado, Linda 38
Tocqueville, Alexis de 93
Todd, Chuck 43
Toe Zaw Latt 6–7, 89
Trump, Donald 13, 18–19, 39, 43–4, 52, 66, 99, 106–7, 118–19, 121
trust in media 88–9, 125
truth 43–6
  see also objectivity

U

undercover investigations 109–10
United Kingdom 29–30, 41, 66, 71, 73, 86, *87*, 88, 97–8, *98*, 100, 101–2, 104, 121, 130, 133
United States 7–12, 13, 18–19, 36–9, *38*, 43–5, 51–9, 66, 67–8, 71, 72, 74–5, 86–7, 93–6, 100, 103, 104, 106–7, 118–21, 127–31, 133

V

Venkiteswaran, Gayathry 32
virtual private networks (VPNs) 140
Voice of America 59

W

Wa Lone 13, 34–5, 113–14, *114*
Wallace, Lewis Raven 53, 57, 103
The Washington Post 54, 58, 74–5
Watson, Morris 53
Wells, Ida B. 57, *57*
West, Bryan 9–11, 67, 68
Westminster Review 24
Whitehead, Laurence 27
Williams, Hannah 85
wire copy 83
Worlds of Journalism survey 28, 40, 44, 59

Y

Ye Htut 32
Ye Naing Moe 113–15, 138
Yong, Ed 72, 73

Z

Ziblatt, Daniel 37

www.ingramcontent.com/pod-product-compliance
Lightning Source LLC
Chambersburg PA
CBHW020415080526
44584CB00014B/1332